Bugs & Slugs

Todd Telander

FALCONGUIDES

GUILFORD, CONNECTICUT
HELENA, MONTANA

AN IMPRINT OF GLOBE PEQUOT PRESS

To my wife, Kirsten; my children, Miles and Oliver; and my parents—
all of whom have supported and encouraged me through the years.

FALCONGUIDES®

Copyright © 2014 Morris Book Publishing, LLC
Illustrations © 2014 Todd Telander

ALL RIGHTS RESERVED. No part of this book may be reproduced or trans-
mitted in any form by any means, electronic or mechanical, including
photocopying and recording, or by any information storage and retrieval
system, except as may be expressly permitted in writing from the pub-
lisher. Requests for permission should be addressed to Globe Pequot
Press, Attn: Rights and Permissions Department, 246 Goose Lane, Suite
200, Guilford, CT 06437.

FalconGuides is an imprint of Globe Pequot Press.
Falcon, FalconGuides, and Outfit Your Mind are registered trademarks of
Morris Book Publishing, LLC.

Illustrations: Todd Telander
Project Editor: Staci Zacharski
Text Design: Sheryl P. Kober
Layout: Sue Murray

Library of Congress Cataloging-in-Publication Data is available on file.

ISBN 978-0-7627-8494-3

Printed in the United States of America

Contents

Crustaceans

Gastropods

Annelids

Myriapods

Introduction

Bugs & Slugs may be a catchy title for this pocket field guide, but it explores the lives of many more kinds of invertebrate animals and is designed to help the novice make sense of how these little creatures are organized into groups. For many of us, the term *bug* is used, often disparagingly, for any small invertebrate that creeps, slithers, burrows, climbs, or flies. But technically, true bugs are only one group of the vast diversity of insects. In addition, we will cover arachnids (including the spiders, ticks, mites, and scorpions), crustaceans (including the sowbugs and crabs), gastropods (including the snails and slugs), annelids (including the earthworms and leeches), and myriapods (including the millipedes and centipedes). The majority of species presented in this book can be found in your backyard, so with some patience, and perhaps a magnifying glass, you can easily learn about and acquaint yourself with a fascinating world that is most often overlooked and misunderstood. You may also find that creatures that were once feared are, when given respect, quite sociable and harmless, and essential components to a healthy ecosystem.

Notes about the Species Accounts

Names

The common name as well as the scientific name are given at the beginning of each entry. Of the two, the universally accepted scientific name of genus and species is the more reliable identifier, because common names tend to vary regionally and sometimes there is more than one, as may be noted in the Description section (see page viii). For those familiar with Latin, scientific names can also provide valuable clues about the species in question. The Dogbane Tiger Moth's scientific name, *Cycnia tenera*, is a good example. *Cycnia* signifies a kind of swan, and *tenera* means soft or delicate. The translation suggests a moth with soft, swan-like coloring, which in fact is the case.

Orders and Classes

Insects and other invertebrates are grouped into orders and classes based on similar structures, behaviors, and common ancestry. In the Order or Class section you'll find both the scientific name and the common one for each animal's group. Once you are familiar with the more common orders and classes and their shared characteristics, you can often place an unfamiliar animal into an order, which will reduce your search to a smaller group.

Size

Sizes given refer to the length of the body, without legs, wings, or antennae. For some winged species, length of wingspan is given, from forewing tip to forewing tip with the wings outstretched. Use these measurements as a general guide to give a sense of the relative size of your subject, noting that there can be quite a bit of variability between different individuals of the same species, and in many cases, between the male and female.

Habitat

Habitat is the general description of the land, climate, and vegetative features within an animal's range. Some are restricted to a very specific habitat, often tied to a certain food plant or climate, while others are quite general in their requirements.

Range

Range is the geographic area where a species exists. It can be very broad, such as the worldwide area inhabited by the Indian-Meal Moth, or quite limited, like the comparatively much smaller area of Southern California, home to the Desert Tarantula. Range is a helpful diagnostic tool because you can quickly note the species that you are likely to encounter in your area. But also be aware that there are cases when individuals carried by winds, or in migration, are found far from their normal range.

Description

The descriptions give plain-language lists of the general features and lifestyles of adults and larvae, though if scientific terms are needed for better accuracy, they'll be included. (Diagrams of scientifically labeled insect parts are provided on page ix.) Within each description you'll find attributes such as body shape and color, style of antennae, hairiness, number of legs, wing shape, general behavior, and feeding habits. In many cases the eggs, larvae, and pupae may also be described.

Illustrations

The illustrations show the upper side of an average specimen of each species. Use them as a visual guide to overall shape, color, and patterning, bearing in mind that there may be considerable variation in appearance among individuals, particularly between males and females, or for species that have distinct forms in different ranges. For some large groups, such as the earthworms or millipedes, only one representative species is illustrated.

Parts of a General Insect

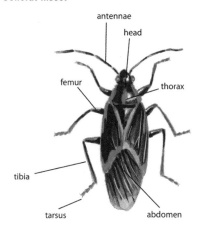

antennae
head
femur
thorax
tibia
tarsus
abdomen

Parts of a Butterfly/Moth

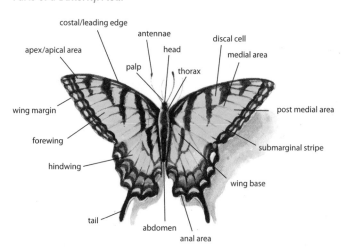

costal/leading edge
apex/apical area
antennae
head
discal cell
medial area
palp
thorax
wing margin
post medial area
forewing
submarginal stripe
hindwing
wing base
tail
abdomen
anal area

Parts of a Spider

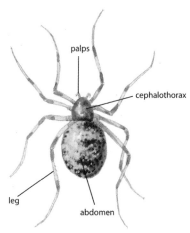

Parts of a Slug

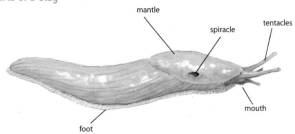

INSECTS

Mayflies (many species)
Order: Ephemeroptera (Mayflies)
Size: ⅛–1" (without tail filaments)
Habitat: Freshwater streams, ponds, shallow lakes, and nearby habitats
Range: Throughout North America

The mayflies comprise a very large group of small, soft-bodied, delicate insects that are active not only in May, but throughout the summer as well. Adults have two pairs (seldom one pair) of thin, triangular wings, with the hindwing substantially smaller than the forewing, and both held closed high over the back when at rest. The abdomen is long and thin, and ends in two or three tail filaments that are up to two times as long as the body. They are generally plainly colored shades of yellow and brown with clear wings (darker in subadults). The nymphs are entirely aquatic, living under submerged rocks and logs for up to four years, molting into terrestrial forms that molt one more time to the mature adults. Adults do not feed and typically live for only one day or less. They are an important food source for many freshwater fish; indeed, many artificial flies used by anglers are made to look like mayflies. The Golden Mayfly adult is illustrated.

Springtails (many species)
Order: Collembola (Springtails)
Size: Up to ⅜"
Habitat: Almost any habitat with sufficient moisture, including soil, leaf litter, tide pools, and snowfields
Range: Throughout North America

The springtails comprise an enormous group of tiny hexapods, with over 3,000 species recognized worldwide. Although difficult to discern as individuals because of their small size and cryptic coloration, they are usually noticed when they occur in huge numbers on the surface of quiet pools, in decaying plant matter or seaweed, and even on snowbanks (where they are known as "snow fleas"). They are wingless, with short, stubby legs, and either have elongated or globular abdomens. They also possess a specialized, forked appendage extending from the lower abdomen (the furcula) that when quickly contracted, thrusts the body into the air (hence the name "springtail"). The color is typically shades of brown or gray, but certain species may be yellow, white, red, or purple. They feed on all manner of small organic material, including fungi, and because of their huge numbers, are extremely important ecologically. A springtail of the elongate-bodied type is illustrated.

Blue-eyed Darner, *Aeshna multicolor*
Order: Odonata (Dragonflies and Damselflies)
Size: Up to 2½"
Habitat: Ponds, streams, wetlands
Range: Western United States

The darners are among the largest and swiftest dragonflies. Their huge compound eyes encompass most of the head and are joined at the top. The abdomen is long and thin, and the four broad wings are transparent and held outspread while at rest. The body is blackish (in males) or brownish (in females), with blue patterning on the abdomen, blue stripes on the thorax, and iridescent bluish-green eyes. The nymphs are also quite large (2" or more) and live in water, feeding on small invertebrates or small fish and tadpoles. Adult Blue-eyed Darners spend most of the day whizzing through the air catching insects in flight. The adult is illustrated.

Green Darner, *Anax junius*
Order: Odonata (Dragonflies and Damselflies)
Size: Up to 3"
Habitat: Ponds, streams, wetlands
Range: Throughout the contiguous United States

The Green Darner is a large dragonfly, similar to the Blue-eyed Darner with its large compound eyes, long and thin abdomen, and four broad, transparent wings that are held outspread while at rest. The thorax is green, and the abdomen is blue (in males) or violet-gray (in females). The eyes are milky brown, and the front of the head has concentric light and dark marks. Most of the day they fly swiftly, catching flying insects. The nymphs are quite large (1¾" long), aquatic, dark brown and green, and feed on aquatic invertebrates, small fish, and tadpoles. After several molts, the nymph crawls ashore and sheds its final skin to emerge as an adult. The adult male is illustrated.

Variegated Meadowhawk, *Sympetrum corruptum*
Order: Odonata (Dragonflies and Damselflies)
Size: Up to 1¾"
Habitat: Ponds, streams, wetlands
Range: Throughout the contiguous United States (more common in the West)

As with other members of this family, the Variegated Meadowhawk has large compound eyes, a long and thin abdomen, tiny antennae, and two pairs of wings of nearly equal size. It also holds its wings spread flat when at rest (unlike damselflies that hold their wings closed over the back). It is relatively dainty for a dragonfly and is colored dark brown or reddish overall, with two yellowish spots on the sides of the thorax and an intricately patterned abdomen. The wings have a pinkish or golden cast and a dark patch near the apex. The nymphs are aquatic, with gills, and feed on aquatic insects. Adults spend most of their time in flight or perched on branches, and prey on flying insects. Northern individuals migrate as far south as Central America in the winter. The adult male is illustrated.

Violet Tail, *Argia fumipennis violacea*
Order: Odonata (Dragonflies and Damselflies)
Size: Up to 1¼"
Habitat: Ponds, streams, lakes with vegetation
Range: Throughout the contiguous United States

The Violet Tail, or Violet Dancer, is one the most common damsel-flies in the United States and southern Canada. These tiny relatives of the dragonflies are characterized by extremely thin, long abdo-mens and generally clear wings with narrow bases that are held together above the back when at rest (although some species do keep their wings apart, but not flat like dragonflies). The Violet Tail is beautifully marked with violet and black (in males) and brown and black (in females). Some individuals of southern races have dark wings. They fly over shallow, weedy waters, catching small insects in the air, and are often seen flying clasped together in male/female pairs. The eggs are laid in the water and hatch into aquatic nymph forms. The adult male is illustrated.

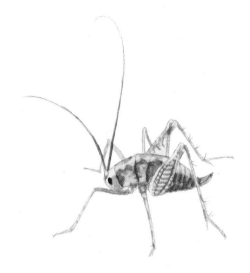

Cave Cricket, *Ceuthophilus maculatus*
Order: Orthoptera (Crickets, Grasshoppers, Katydids, and Mantids)
Size: Up to ¾"
Habitat: A wide variety of moist, dark places; under rocks and logs, caves
Range: Eastern and central North America

The Cave Cricket is part of the group known as the "camel crickets" because of its distinctive, rounded or humped back on its squat body. This cricket lacks wings and has massive rear legs and extremely long, thin antennae. Its color is light brown with darker brown spotting and mottling across the back, and dark brown striations on the lower part of the hind legs (indeed, its other common name is the Spotted Camel Cricket). Hiding during the day in sheltered, dark retreats, Cave Crickets become active at night to feed on a wide variety of plant or animal matter with their well-developed, chewing mouthparts. They are unable to produce the trilling sounds of the true crickets.

Field Crickets (many species)

Order: Orthoptera (Crickets, Grasshoppers, Katydids, and Mantids)
Size: Up to 1"
Habitat: A wide variety of moist habitats; brush, leaf litter, under rocks and logs
Range: Throughout North America

The term "field cricket" has been applied to several different species, all of which are quite similar in appearance. They have a somewhat flattened body, tough wings, long and thin antennae, large rear legs, and a pair of forked appendages (cerci) that protrude from the end of the abdomen. In females there is also a long, tubular structure (the ovipositor) through which eggs are laid. They are almost always black, unlike the paler color of house crickets. Field crickets scurry through underbrush and moist places during the night, feeding on a wide variety of plant or invertebrate prey, including eggs of other insects. During mid-summer the males begin their familiar, high-pitched trilling calls caused by rubbing a specialized part of the wing. This attracts females, who will deposit eggs in the soil or in plant tissue.

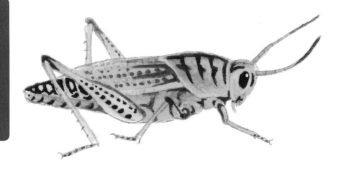

Eastern Lubber Grasshopper, *Romalea microptera*
Order: Orthoptera (Crickets, Grasshoppers, Katydids, and Mantids)
Size: Up to 2½"
Habitat: Fields, rural gardens, disturbed areas
Range: Southeastern United States

The Eastern Lubber Grasshopper is one of many members of the group known as "short-horned grasshoppers" due to their relatively short, stubby antennae. The body has a long abdomen and shield-like upper thorax (pronotum), the eyes are large, and the mouth has strong, chewing mouthparts. Although equipped with large hind legs like other grasshoppers and crickets, it is not a particularly good jumper, but rather it lumbers sluggishly along the ground and vegetation. Also, because its wings are so short, it is incapable of flight. The color may be yellow to reddish brown with intricate black markings, or nearly solid black with a yellow edging on the back of the pronotum and on the abdomen. These large plant-eaters can occur in huge numbers and are often considered pests to farmers and gardeners. A light-phase adult is illustrated.

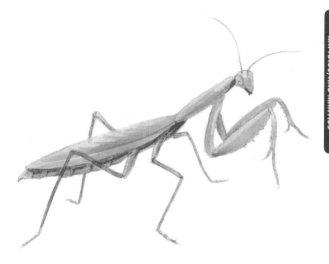

Praying Mantis, *Mantis religiosa*
Order: Orthoptera (Crickets, Grasshoppers, Katydids, and Mantids)
Size: Up to 2½"
Habitat: Gardens, fields
Range: Eastern and northwestern United States

Also known as the European Mantis, the Praying Mantis was introduced to North America from Europe in the late 1800s and is now common and welcome in gardens and flowerbeds across the United States. This is a long, slender insect with thin legs, an extended thorax region, and a relatively small, triangular head with big eyes and lacy antennae. Most obvious are the large, spined forelegs with a longer than usual inner segment. The color can range from green to brownish, with a dark ringed spot on the inner part of the foreleg base. Praying Mantises hunt by waiting motionless with the front legs raised in a "praying" position, then quickly grasping prey when it is in range. All manner of insects, their larvae, and spiders are eaten, including other mantids. Females create a papery egg case on twigs, which overwinters and produces a hundred or more tiny young in the spring.

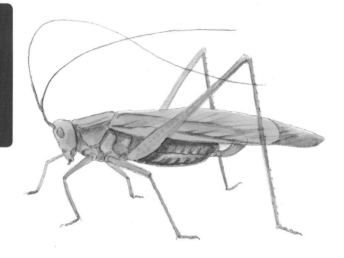

Fork-tailed Bush Katydid, *Scudderia furcata*
Order: Orthoptera (Crickets, Grasshoppers, Katydids, and Mantids)
Size: Up to 2"
Habitat: Fields, brush, woodland edges, parks
Range: Throughout North America

The Fork-tailed Bush Katydid is in a group known as the "long-horned grasshoppers" because of its long, wispy antennae. It is a fairly large grasshopper with a plump abdomen and wings that extend well beyond the hind end. The rear legs are much longer than the two front pair, but the basal portion is thinner than in other grasshoppers. The male has a forked abdominal tip (hence the common name), while the female has a bladelike ovipositor at the tip. The color is generally a uniform grass green, but rarely can be reddish or pink. Males are equipped with structures on the forewing that produce a series of dry, lisping chirps. Eggs, which are small, oval, and flat, are laid on leaves in a distinctive overlapping pattern. There, they overwinter and hatch into juveniles in the spring. The female is illustrated.

Jerusalem Cricket, *Stenopelmatus fuscus*
Order: Orthoptera (Crickets, Grasshoppers, Katydids, and Mantids)
Size: Up to 2"
Habitat: Dark, moist places in soil, leaf litter, under rocks, etc.
Range: Western United States

Although fearsome in appearance, the Jerusalem Cricket is not poisonous or dangerous, although it has been known to deliver a mild bite if threatened. Looking almost like a fat, oversize ant, it also goes by a number of common names, including "old bald-headed man," "child of the earth," "skull insect," and "potato bug." The abdomen is plump and clearly segmented; the head is large, round, and smooth with beady black eyes; and the limbs are compact and have spines to aid in digging. Wings are absent. The color is glossy amber-brown with dark brown bands over the abdomen. These crickets are active mostly at night, feeding on decaying organic matter on the ground, burrowing into the soil for plant tubers, or wandering into homes. It can make a hissing sound by rubbing the back legs against the body, or a thumping sound by tapping its abdomen against the ground.

American Cockroach, *Periplaneta americana*
Order: Blattodea (Cockroaches and Termites)
Size: Up to 2"
Habitat: Woodlands of subtropical habitats, urban areas, buildings, sewers
Range: Worldwide

Although an important insect in the subtropical ecosystems where it lives wild, the American Cockroach is best known as a creepy pest that inhabits nooks and crevices of homes and other buildings throughout North America. The body is oval shaped and flattened, with overlapping wings that cover the entire back (wings are larger in males than in females). The head is small and usually obscured by the large pronotus (front of the thorax), and the antennae are thin and longer than the body. Two appendages at the rear (cerci) are well developed. The color is reddish brown overall, with a paler band across the pronotum. Cockroaches are active mostly during the night, crawling and sometimes flying in search of almost any food source. In the wild they seek out hidden places under rocks and logs; in buildings their flattened shape allows them to squeeze into the thinnest spaces between wood panels and cement walls.

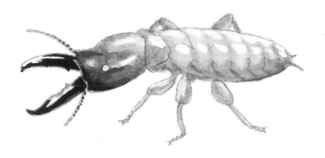

Pacific Coast Termite, *Zootermopsis angusticollis*
Order: Blattodea (Termites)
Size: Up to 1"
Habitat: Moist woodlands around stumps, fallen trees, wooden structures
Range: Western United States

The Pacific Coast Termite is a member of the "rotting wood termites" group because it needs moist wood to exist. These termites are also known as "white ants" because of their superficial resemblance to ants. They form highly social, organized colonies that contain reproductive members (the largest), soldiers (for defense), and young who serve as workers. In general, they are soft-bodied, whitish, with no dramatic indent between the thorax and the abdomen (as in in ants). Individuals who become reproductive forms are brownish and have wings, while soldiers are pale with dark brown heads and enlarged pincers. They feed on rotting wood, the cellulose of which is digested by microorganisms in their intestines. They can occasionally be destructive to older wood structures but are most common in the wild, where they are important as decomposers of organic material. The soldier form is illustrated.

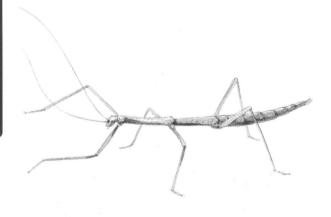

Northern Walkingstick, *Diapheromera femorata*
Order: Phasmatodea (Walkingsticks)
Size: Up to 3½"
Habitat: Deciduous woodlands, gardens, parks
Range: Central and eastern United States

Also known as the Common American Walkingstick, these curious insects are uncanny in their resemblance to twigs, sticks, and vines as they stand motionless or even sway gently to mimic a breeze. This camouflage allows them to remain virtually undetected to predators, especially when the limbs are held close to the body. As a further defense, they can detach a limb, which regenerates in a subsequent molt. The body is elongate and tubular, like a twig, with a small squarish head and very thin, long legs. Wings are absent. The color is brown (in males), brown with a bit of green (in females), or overall green (in juveniles). Walkingsticks feed on the leaves of deciduous trees and shrubs, mostly at night for safety, slowly munching an entire leaf before moving on to the next. Their bizarre appearance and gentle nature have made them popular as pets. The male is illustrated.

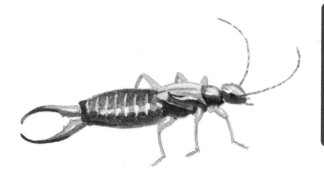

European Earwig, *Forficula auricularia*
Order: Dermaptera (Earwigs)
Size: Up to ⅝"
Habitat: Variable habitats with moist, dark hiding places; gardens, fields
Range: Northern United States

Many people are squeamish around earwigs, but their fears are unfounded, as these insects are perfectly harmless to humans. They do not crawl into people's ears, and the pincers at the rear end are used as self-defense against small predators but are much too weak to harm humans. The European Earwig was introduced from Europe and now inhabits most temperate climates of the United States. The body is elongate, dark reddish brown above and yellowish below and on the legs and antennae. The hind pincers are robust and curved in males, but relatively straight and thin in females. Short wings are present, but these earwigs rarely fly. They are active mostly at night, when they search for bits of plants or small insects in leaf litter, the soil, or up the stems of plants. Occasionally they will find their way into homes through small cracks and feed on foods therein. The male is illustrated.

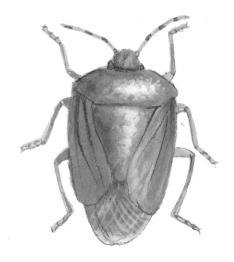

Green Stink Bug, *Acrosternum hilare*
Order: Hemiptera (True bugs)
Size: Up to ¾"
Habitat: Woodlands, gardens, meadows
Range: Throughout North America

The Green Stink Bug is a member of the order of "true bugs" (Hemiptera), all of which have forewings that fold neatly over the back and are leathery at the basal half and membranous at the outer half. There is also a triangular patch on the top of the thorax between the wings. The body is broad and flattened, like a little shield, with small legs and a small head. It is overall bright green, often edged with yellow or red along the body's perimeter, and has black bands on the antennae. It uses well-developed sucking mouthparts to extract the juices of all kinds of plant material, including commercial crops and home gardens, where it can be a major pest. The common name is due to the fact that adults and larvae can emit a foul-smelling fluid in defense.

Boxelder Bug, *Boisea trivittata*
Order: Hemiptera (True bugs)
Size: Up to ½"
Habitat: Deciduous woodlands with trees of the maple family and nearby fields
Range: Throughout North America

The Boxelder Bug is another of our true bugs, with the characteristic X-shaped pattern on the back formed from the overlapping wings and a triangular top section of the thorax. The body is elongate, tapering to a small head, and has fairly long legs and antennae. It is black or dark brown with red-orange marks on the forewings and thorax. Nymphs are like smaller adults but uniformly bright red. These bugs are often found in large, unorganized aggregations soaking up the sunlight. They feed on seeds, fruits, and the leaves of box elder, ash, and a variety of maples by piercing with a specialized beak and sucking out the juices. They are generally not considered pests, but in cold seasons they may migrate into homes in large numbers. Although in a separate family than the stink bugs, they can emit a foul odor if disturbed.

Harlequin Bug, *Murgantia histrionica*
Order: Hemiptera (True bugs)
Size: Up to ⅜"
Habitat: Fields, gardens, meadows
Range: Lower latitudes throughout the United States

The Harlequin Bug is a member of the group known as "stink bugs" because of the foul-smelling odor they emit. Also known as "cabbage bugs" or "fire bugs," they are broad, short, and shaped like a small shield. The upperside is attractively patterned in yellow-orange and deep black, and the folded wings produce the traditional X shape across the abdomen (common to the Hemiptera, or true bugs). Tiny eggs are laid in rows on the underside of leaves and look like black-and-white-ringed barrels. Growing nymphs and adults suck the sap of many garden and crop plants such as cabbage, mustard, tomatoes, and beets, often causing serious damage.

Water Boatman, *Corixa* spp.
Order: Hemiptera (True bugs)
Size: Up to ½"
Habitat: Ponds, streams
Range: Throughout North America

Water boatmen are aquatic members of the true bug group that can be found in almost any body of stagnant fresh or brackish water, including swimming pools, birdbaths, and puddles. The body is elongate and oval with a flattened, streamlined shape, and the small antennae fold neatly into grooves on the head. The front legs are reduced, while the rear legs are enlarged, with feathery outer sections that serve as paddles for forward propulsion. The color is pale to dark gray-brown with many thin, black transverse striations. Water boatmen dart through the water near the bottom or cling to aquatic plants. They feed on algae or bits of detritus, using their small front legs as a scoop. They are capable of making high-pitched chirps by rubbing their forelegs against their head. Unlike another group of aquatic bugs, the backswimmers, water boatmen do not bite people.

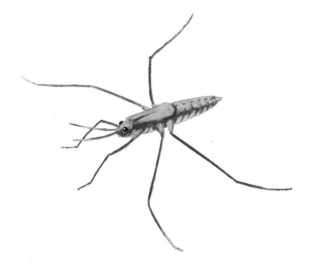

Common Water Strider, *Aquarius remigis*
Order: Hemiptera (True bugs)
Size: Up to ½"
Habitat: Ponds, streams, wetlands
Range: Throughout North America

Water striders, as a group, are fascinating aquatic bugs that are almost always in motion, darting across the surface of shallow waters. Sometimes called "skaters" or "Jesus bugs," they can literally walk on water by using excellent weight distribution of their legs, which are lined with tiny water-repelling hairs, and the physics of surface tension. The Common Water Strider is relatively small with a narrow blackish body, a pair of short grasping legs, and very long, thin middle and hind legs. They eat a variety of planktonic food and are capable of subduing larger insects as well, which they suck the juices from with specialized mouthparts.

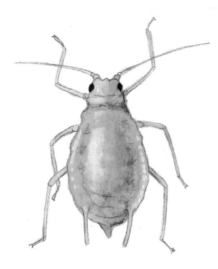

Green Peach Aphid, *Myzus persicae*
Order: Homoptera (Aphids, cicadas, and allies)
Size: Up to ⅛"
Habitat: Orchards, gardens near trees in the peach family, including plum, cherry, and apricot
Range: Throughout North America

Aphids comprise a group of thousands of species throughout the world. They are typically quite small with soft bodies, thin legs, long antennae, a taillike appendage, and tubular growths called cornicles on either side of the back. The Green Peach Aphid is yellowish green, but winged forms are also black on the head and thorax. They feed on sap in plant tissue of a wide variety of garden plants and trees by inserting a specialized sucking mouthpart called a stylet, and discharge a sticky, sugary fluid known as honeydew. Because of their ability to reproduce asexually, populations can grow very fast and become major pests. However, they are an important food source for many other insects, especially ladybird beetles and their larvae. Some aphid colonies are tended by ants, who protect them in exchange for a constant supply of honeydew.

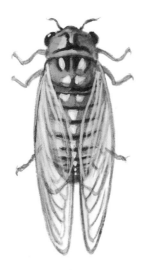

Grand Western Cicada, *Tibicen dorsatus*
Order: Homoptera (Aphids, Cicadas, and Allies)
Size: Up to 1½"
Habitat: Woodlands, fields, rural gardens
Range: Southwestern and central United States

Cicadas are large, chunky insects with bulbous eyes, tiny legs, and two pairs of membranous, thick-veined wings that are much longer than the body. The Grand Western Cicada, also known as the "bush cicada" or "grassland cicada," is handsomely marked in patterns of black, brown, and white, with clear wings that have brownish veins. The wings are held angled, tentlike, when at rest. Male cicadas are capable of producing a surprisingly loud buzz or whining sound with specialized organs under their abdomens, and most commonly do so late in the day during the late summer months. The nymphs, after hatching, burrow into the ground and feed on plant roots, and can live for several years in this stage. Eventually they emerge and molt on a nearby tree trunk to become the mature adults, who live only a few weeks. The empty shells of the final molt are often seen clinging to bark.

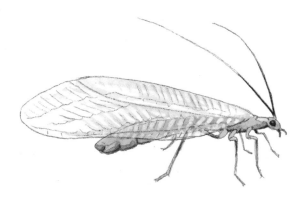

Green Lacewings, *Chrysopa* spp.

Order: Neuroptera (Lacewings and Antlions)
Size: Up to ⅝"
Habitat: Gardens, fields
Range: Throughout North America

Green lacewings are a group of dainty, large-winged insects that are common in home gardens and weedy fields. The body is bright green and elongate, with an especially long abdomen, delicate legs, and a small head with metallic golden-brown eyes. The wings are much longer than the body and clear, with lacey, greenish veins. The larvae are wingless and armed with ferocious-looking front pincers. Adults may often be seen at night, as they are attracted, like moths, to lights. Larvae and adults are predators of small, soft-bodied insects, especially aphids, which they devour with chewing mouthparts. Although slightly foul smelling, they are very beneficial in gardens and greenhouses to control aphid populations. Curiously, their tiny eggs are attached to foliage via a long, thin, dangling stalk.

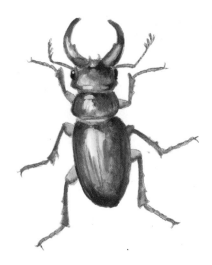

Reddish-brown Stag Beetle, *Lucanus capreolus*
Order: Coleoptera (Beetles)
Size: Up to 1¼"
Habitat: Woodlands, rural and urban areas with decaying wood
Range: Eastern United States

Beetles are by far the largest group of insects, with over 300,000 described species. They are noted for the hardened or leathery forewings that meet at a central line down the middle of the back, covering the membranous hindwings that are used for flight. The stag beetle is a robust member of the group, with a wide head, bent antennae, and formidable, toothed mandibles (larger in males) that are used in breeding battles with other stag beetles. The Reddish-brown Stag Beetle is uniformly shiny dark reddish brown with yellow-orange bases to the legs. The larvae use chewing mouthparts to feed on rotting wood, while adults feed on sap and wood juices. Adults fly during the night and are commonly attracted to lights.

Convergent Ladybird Beetle, *Hippodamia convergens*
Order: Coleoptera (Beetles)
Size: Up to ⅜"
Habitat: Gardens, fields, woodlands
Range: Eastern United States

The ladybird beetles, commonly called "ladybugs" (although they are not true bugs), comprise a large group of familiar and welcome beetles that are voracious predators on many destructive insects such as aphids and scale insects. Most are small, nearly round and domed above, have tiny legs and antennae, and are colored orange to reddish with variable black spots. The Convergent Ladybird Beetle is shiny red with thirteen black spots on the back and has a black pronotum (top of the thorax) with a white border and two converging white stripes. The larva is spindly, spiny, and black with orange spots, and it forms a pupa that is orangey with black spots. Adults may overwinter in large numbers under clumps of leaves, becoming active again in the spring. Ladybird beetles are sometimes bought and released as a biological pest-control device in gardens and crops.

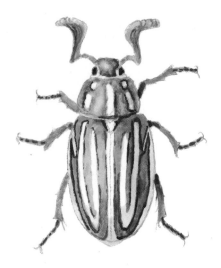

Ten-lined June Beetle, *Polyphylla decemlineata*
Order: Coleoptera (Beetles)
Size: Up to 1½"
Habitat: Woodlands, fields, gardens
Range: Western United States

The Ten-lined June Beetle is a member of a large group known as the "scarab beetles," all relatively large and robust with big heads, powerful front legs for digging, and curious, platelike antennae that can be fanned out or folded into a compact ball. It is mottled golden brown and black above, with distinct white lines along the shell-like forewings on the back and on the thorax. The underside is lined with fuzzy tan or reddish hairs. The larva is pale, grub-like, curved into a C shape, lives underground, and can be a serious pest where it feeds on the roots of plants or young trees. Adults are most active at night in warm weather, flying low over fields, and are attracted to lights.

Common Black Ground Beetle, *Pterostichus melanarius*
Order: Coleoptera (Beetles)
Size: Up to ⅝"
Habitat: Gardens, woodlands, fields
Range: Throughout North America

Ground beetles are members of the family Carabidae (known as the "carab beetles") and consist of thousands of species. Most are shiny black or of iridescent colors with prominent thoraxes, long and thin legs, and narrow heads. Although capable of flight, they typically speed away on foot rather than fly when threatened. The Common Black Ground Beetle was introduced from Europe and is now common in much of North America. Its color is glossy black overall, and the forewings, folded neatly over the back, are grooved. They spend the day hiding under stones and logs and become active at night, pursuing small insects and slugs on the ground or on plants. They are generally considered beneficial in gardens and crops, although they can emit a foul-smelling substance if handled.

Three-lined Potato Beetle, *Lema triloneata*
Order: Coleoptera (Beetles)
Size: Up to ¼"
Habitat: Areas with plants of the nightshade family (Solanaceae); fields, crops, gardens
Range: Throughout North America

Three-lined Potato Beetles are members of a group known as the "leaf beetles," with over 1,000 species worldwide. Like all beetles, they have a pair of tough, leathery wings that cover the membranous flight wings underneath. Although destructive, they are attractive small insects with an overall orangey coloration, three black stripes along the back, black eyes and antennae, and sometimes two black spots on the thorax. The bases of the legs are orange and the outer portions are black. Larvae and adults feed almost exclusively on plants of the nightshade family, especially potatoes, and can be a serious pest in crops and gardens. Because of toxins in these plants, the beetles are distasteful to most predators, and the larvae are even less attractive because they cover themselves with a mucous-like covering of excrement.

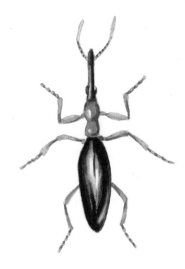

Sweet Potato Weevil, *Cylas formicarius*
Order: Coleoptera (Beetles)
Size: Up to ¼"
Habitat: Areas with plants in the Convolvulaceae family, including sweet potato and morning glory
Range: Southeastern United States

The Sweet Potato Weevil is a member of a very large family of beetles known as the "snout beetles" or "weevils," characterized by a thin, elongate snout projection from the head. This quite unusual-looking species is relatively thin and elongate, with a metallic blue-black abdomen, red-orange thorax and legs, and a black head and snout. The larvae are cream colored and wormlike, passing through several molting stages before reaching adult form. They can be a significant pest on crops of sweet potatoes, as they bore through stems, roots, and tubers, aided by their long snouts, causing decay and disease.

Pyralis Firefly, *Photinus pyralis*
Order: Coleoptera (Beetles)
Size: Up to ½"
Habitat: Meadows, swamps
Range: Eastern and Central United States

Fireflies, also known as "lightning bugs," are actually a kind of small beetle. They are most active on spring and summer nights, when they delight viewers with blinking flashes of light, the pattern of which varies with different species. A special chemical process in the last sections of the abdomen creates this yellow-green glow, and it is found in the larvae as well. The body is soft and elongate, with small legs and a large pronotum (top of the thorax) that conceals the head when seen from above. The back is black with thin, orange stripes down the center and sides. The pronotum is yellow around the edges with a red interior, and has a black mark in the center. Adults rarely feed, but larvae prey on small insects, slugs, and worms, which they find under logs and in moist leaf litter.

Eyed Click Beetle, *Alaus oculatus*
Order: Coleoptera (Beetles)
Size: Up to 1½"
Habitat: Deciduous woodlands, orchards
Range: Eastern United States

The click beetles have a curious, hinge-like apparatus in the thorax that can be snapped quickly (producing the *click* sound), sending the beetles into the air. In this way they can right themselves if they become inverted. The body is elongate and somewhat flat, with small legs and a large thorax that has pointed sections on the rear sides. The Eyed Click Beetle is so called because of two prominent black spots bordered by white (the eye spots) on the thorax, thought to deter predators. The abdomen is black, ridged, and speckled with white dots. They are found mostly around areas of rotting wood and tree trunks. Larvae, known as "wire worms," are hard and shiny, live in the soil, eat mostly the roots of plants, and can be a major pest to crops. Adults eat little but occasionally feed on flower nectar.

Pipevine Swallowtail, *Battus philenor*
Order: Lepidoptera (Butterflies and Moths)
Size: Wingspan 3–5"
Habitat: Woodland edges, streamsides, open fields
Range: Southern latitudes across the contiguous United States and into Mexico

The Pipevine Swallowtail is a dark, medium-size, active swallow-tail with shallowly scalloped hindwings and moderate tail projections. It is poisonous to predators and thus often mimicked by other butterfly species. The upperside of the forewing is flat black and iridescent, while the upper surface of the hindwing is metallic blue (more developed in males) with pale crescent-shaped spots along its base. The underside hindwing has large, orange, submarginal spots and retains the blue sheen of its upper surface. The body is black with small yellow spots along the sides, and the antennae are thin with clubbed tips. The caterpillar is dark, reddish brown, smooth, and lined with fleshy appendages and orange spots. The caterpillar eats the leaves of pipevines and related plants. The adult feeds on flower nectar and nutrients from mud puddles.

Black Swallowtail, *Papilio polyxenes*
Order: Lepidoptera (Butterflies and Moths)
Size: Wingspan 3–4"
Habitat: Roadsides, sunny fields, meadows
Range: Throughout the contiguous United States

The Black Swallowtail is a common dark butterfly with prominent tails and scalloped hindwing margins. The wings are black overall with a prominent, broken, postmedial band of yellow and yellow spotting along the margins. The lower hindwings are iridescent blue (more pronounced in females), each showing an anal spot that is orange with a black center. The wing undersides are marked similarly, but the spotting is more orange than yellow, especially on the hindwings. The body is plump and black, with rows of small yellow spots down the abdomen. The antennae are thin with clubbed tips. The caterpillar is smooth, plump, and green with orange-spotted black bands. The caterpillar eats the leaves of cow parsnip, Queen Anne's lace, and other plants in the carrot family. Adults feed on nectar from flowers.

Eastern Tiger Swallowtail, *Papilio glaucus*
Order: Lepidoptera (Butterflies and Moths)
Size: Wingspan 3–5½"
Habitat: Gardens, parks, riversides, forest clearings
Range: Throughout eastern United States

Among the largest of North American butterflies, the Eastern Tiger Swallowtail is common throughout its range, is diurnal, and—typical of this family—has distinct projections, or "tails," on the hindwings. When alighted and/or feeding, the wings may be seen to tremble. Both sexes are bright yellow above and show ragged black stripes, like those of a tiger, along the anterior forewings and black marginal patterning on both fore- and hindwings. The first submarginal spot on the hindwing is orange. The underside is patterned similarly but is much paler yellow. Females show bright blue posterior markings, and in some southern individuals may be nearly black overall (and look similar to the Spicebush Swallowtail). Like the wings, the body has black and yellow stripes. The caterpillar is brown to greenish, smooth, and plump. The caterpillar eats the leaves of trees, including those from the rose, magnolia, laurel, and willow families. Adults feed on flower nectar and the salts and moisture from puddles. The adult female is illustrated.

Orange Sulfur, *Colias eurytheme*
Order: Lepidoptera (Butterflies and Moths)
Size: Wingspan 1½–2½"
Habitat: Meadows, fields, farmlands, roadsides
Range: Throughout the contiguous United States

Also known as the Alfalfa Butterfly, this common butterfly is often found in dense, low-flying groups over alfalfa fields, where it is often considered a pest. The upperside wings are yellow and extensively washed with bright orange. A wide, dark band occurs along the outer margins of both fore- and hindwings, a reddish discal spot appears on the hindwing, and a distinct black discal spot sits on the forewing. The dark margin in females is broken by irregular orange markings. The underside is yellow with a red-bordered white discal spot on the hindwing, accompanied by a smaller spot just above it. The body is pale yellow below, darker above, and the club-tipped antennae are reddish. The caterpillar is thin, smooth, and green, with a pale longitudinal stripe down each side. This species is similar to the Clouded, or Common, Sulfur, which has a lemon yellow rather than orange cast and lacks the hindwing spot. The caterpillar eats alfalfa and clover. Adults feed on flower nectar. The illustration shows the adult male.

Cabbage Butterfly, *Pieris rapae*
Order: Lepidoptera (Butterflies and Moths)
Size: Wingspan 1⅜–1¾"
Habitat: Open fields, farmlands, roadsides
Range: Throughout the contiguous United States

Also known as the Cabbage White or Small White, the Cabbage Butterfly is a hardy, nonnative species introduced to North America in the late 1800s and now found across the continent. The upperside wings are plain, creamy white with gray to black apical patches and show a distinct dark spot on the center of the forewings and upper margins of the hindwings. Females have an additional spot on the forewing, below the first. The underside is pale yellow to yellow-green. Early broods of this species tend to be paler with fewer dark markings than late broods. The body is dark above, paler below, with long hairs, especially on the thorax. The antennae are thin and club-tipped. The caterpillar is pale green with thin, longitudinal yellow stripes and a delicate, bumpy-hairy surface. The caterpillar eats cabbage and other plants of the mustard (Brassicaceae) family, including *Nasturtium* sp. Also known as a "cabbage worm," it is considered a major pest to crops. Adults feed on flower nectar. The illustration depicts the adult female.

Southern Dogface, *Zerene cesonia*
Order: Lepidoptera (Butterflies and Moths)
Size: Wingspan 2–3"
Habitat: Dry fields, open woodlands, farmlands
Range: Coast to coast of mostly southern continental United States, but reaching as far north as the Great Lakes region

The Southern Dogface is a striking sulfur butterfly with rapid flight, pointed wingtips, and straight outer margins to the forewings. It is similar to the California Dogface, which is restricted to a small range in western California. The male is yellow overall with broad black patches at the base and outer margin of its forewings, which also show a black discal spot. These markings together give the crude appearance of the head of a poodle-like dog. The hindwing has a black outer marginal band with two faint, white, orange-bordered spots near the center. The female is a plain, dull yellow with black forewing spots and may show pinkish patterning on her underside hindwing. The body is mottled yellow and black, darker above than below, and has thin, club-tipped antennae. The caterpillar is smooth, green, and variably marked with yellow and black rings and/or whitish longitudinal stripes down each side, with an overall covering of small, blackish warts. The caterpillar eats clover, false indigo, and other plants of the pea family (Fabaceae). Adults feed on flower nectar. The illustration shows the adult male.

American Copper, *Lycaena phlaeas*
Order: Lepidoptera (Butterflies and Moths)
Size: Wingspan 1–1¼"
Habitat: Meadows, roadsides, fields
Range: Throughout the contiguous United States, but most commonly in the northern and eastern regions

The American Copper is a small, beautiful, common butterfly with a fairly aggressive disposition. The wing patterning is variable, but generally the upperside forewing is coppery orange with a dark marginal band and several black spots. The hindwing is mostly blackish or dark brown with an orange basal band. A thin, pale margin is present on both sets of wings. The underside wings are similar but much paler overall. The sexes are similar, although some females may show bluish markings above the orange band on the hindwing. The body is dark brown above, pale grayish below, with dark, club-tipped antennae dotted with white. The caterpillar is slug-like, variously colored pale greenish to reddish and covered with fine hairs. The caterpillar feeds on various sorrels and docks. Adults feed on flower nectar. The adult female is illustrated.

Gray Hairstreak, *Strymon melinus*
Order: Lepidoptera (Butterflies and Moths)
Size: Wingspan 1–1¼"
Habitat: Fields, open rural areas, disturbed sites
Range: Throughout the contiguous United States

The swift-flying Gray Hairstreak is the most common hairstreak in North America. Hairstreaks are so called because of the usual presence of thin streaks along the undersides of the wings. They also usually have one or two thin tails on each hindwing. The upperside wings are overall slate gray (browner in females) with white margins. When there are two tails, they are uneven in length and accompanied near their base by a large orange spot above a smaller black dot. The underside is pale brown-gray with black streaking, bordered with white and orange. The body is stout, grayish above and paler gray below, and has black-and-white-dotted antennae tipped with orange. The caterpillar is pale green to brownish, plump, and covered with fine whitish hairs. The caterpillar eats the fruits, flowers, leaves, and seedpods of a variety of plants, including legumes, mallow, and cotton, often boring into its food. Adults feed on flower nectar. The illustration shows the adult male.

Monarch, *Danaus plexippus*
Order: Lepidoptera (Butterflies and Moths)
Size: Wingspan 3–4½"
Habitat: Sunny, open fields as well as meadows and gardens; during migration, can be found in almost any environment
Range: Throughout the contiguous United States to north-central Mexico

The Monarch is a large, sturdy, long-lived butterfly best known for one of the most incredible migratory journeys of the animal kingdom—its yearly flight to Mexico, in which millions of this species gather in discrete, isolated locations. The uppersides of the wings are deep orange with wide, black stripes along the veins and black margins infused with a double row of white spots. Males have narrower black vein markings than females, as well as a small, dark "sex spot" near the base of each hindwing. The underside is marked as above, but the orange is paler. The body is black with white spots on the head and thorax, with thin, club-tipped antennae. The caterpillar is fat and smooth; is ringed with black, white, and yellow bands; and has black tentacles behind the head. The caterpillar eats leaves and flowers of milkweed. Adults feed on flower nectar. Both store toxins from milkweed that make them distasteful to predators. The adult male is shown.

Red-spotted Purple, *Limenitis arthemis*
Order: Lepidoptera (Butterflies and Moths)
Size: Wingspan 2½–3¾"
Habitat: Deciduous woodlands
Range: Throughout eastern United States

The Red-spotted Purple is the same species as the White Admiral, which has a very different color pattern and ranges farther north, although the two may hybridize to create intermediate forms where their ranges overlap. The Red-spotted Purple superficially resembles the Pipevine Swallowtail, but lacks the tails. The upperside wings are dark blue to black, fading to iridescent blue or blue-green near the margins and most of the hindwing. There are reddish spots along the apex of the forewing. The underside is bluish to brown, with several black-bordered orange spots. The body is a dark blue-gray marked with white underneath. The caterpillar, like that of the Viceroy, is often said to resemble a bird dropping: It is cream colored, mottled with dull brown or gray, and lumpy, and has two thick tentacles. The caterpillar eats the leaves of a variety of trees including wild cherry, willow, poplar, oak, and hawthorn. Adults feed on rotting fruit, dung, and moist soils.

Red Admiral, *Vanessa atalanta*
Order: Lepidoptera (Butterflies and Moths)
Size: Wingspan 1¾–2½"
Habitat: A wide variety of open habitats, especially moist areas
Range: Throughout the contiguous United States

The Red Admiral is not technically an admiral, but a member of the "ladies" or "thistle butterflies" group. The upperside wings are a deep velvety brownish black with orange (not red) medial bands and white apical spots on the forewings and broad, orange marginal bands on the hindwings. Individuals of spring broods are lighter overall, while those of fall broods are darker. The underside of the forewing is similar to its upperside, while the underside of the hindwing is cryptically mottled with grays. The body is black overall, with club-tipped antennae ending with light dots. The caterpillar varies from pale green to blackish, is covered with tiny white spots, and has many branched spines. The caterpillar eats the leaves of plants in the nettle family (Urticaceae). Adults feed on flower nectar (especially thistles), tree sap, moisture from soil, and rotting fruit. The illustration shows the adult's darker "fall" form.

Painted Lady, *Vanessa cardui*
Order: Lepidoptera (Butterflies and Moths)
Size: Wingspan 2–2½"
Habitat: Open habitats, gardens, fields, alpine meadows
Range: Throughout the contiguous United States

The Painted Lady is a medium-size, wide-ranging, common butterfly that can be found around the world, so it is sometimes called the Cosmopolitan. It has strong but erratic flight and is capable of long migrations. The upperside wings are pale orange-brown with extensive black markings. A black apical region on the forewing contains several white spots, and small blue spots may be visible at the inner base of the hindwing. The underside forewing is patterned as above, but the hindwing is mottled in earth tones with a row of submarginal eyespots. The body is speckled light and dark brown above, is whitish below, and has thin, club-tipped antennae ending in pale dots. The caterpillar is blackish with pale yellow stripes, and is covered in fine hairs and bristles. The caterpillar eats a wide variety of plants, including thistles, nettles, burdock, hollyhock, and mallow, enabling it to thrive in most areas. Adults feed on flower nectar.

Buckeye, *Junonia coenia*
Order: Lepidoptera (Butterflies and Moths)
Size: Wingspan 1¾–2½"
Habitat: Open fields, meadows, coastal shores
Range: Throughout the contiguous United States, most commonly in southern latitudes

The Buckeye is a medium-size, common butterfly with pronounced eyespots, which are thought to confuse and deter predators. It tends to remain on or near the ground or low parts of vegetation. The upperside wings are variable shades of brown, with each wing showing one large and one small multicolored spot. There is also a creamy bar near the apex of the forewing, two orange marks in the discal cell, and scalloped patterning along the entire wing edge. The underside is paler, sometimes achieving a rose cast, with eyespots still visible. The body is tan to dark brown with pale, club-tipped antennae. The caterpillar is mottled black, white, and brown, with dark stripes above, and is covered in black branched spines. The caterpillar eats the leaves, buds, and fruit of plantains, gerardias, and snapdragons. Adults feed on flower nectar and moisture from mud and sand.

Mourning Cloak, *Nymphalis antiopa*
Order: Lepidoptera (Butterflies and Moths)
Size: Wingspan 2¼–3½"
Habitat: Deciduous woodlands, parks, rural gardens
Range: Throughout temperate North America

The Mourning Cloak is a common butterfly with the angular, jagged wing margins typical of the tortoiseshells. The adult overwinters in tree cavities, emerging the following spring to breed. The upperside wings are deep burgundy-brown with wide, pale yellow margins. Inside the margin are light blue spots surrounded by black. The underside is dark gray with the same yellowish margin, though on this side it is speckled with black. The body is stout and dark brown to blackish both above and below, with thin, club-tipped antennae. The caterpillar is black, is covered with spines, and has small white dots and a row of reddish spots along the back. The caterpillar eats the leaves of a variety of broadleaf trees, including willow, poplar, elm, birch, and hackberry. Adults feed on rotting fruit, tree sap, flower nectar (rarely), and moisture and salts from soil.

Variable Checkerspot, *Euphydryas chalcedona*
Order: Lepidoptera (Butterflies and Moths)
Size: Wingspan 1¼–2¼"
Habitat: A wide range of habitats including deserts, coastal areas, and mountains
Range: Throughout western contiguous United States, including the Rocky Mountains

The Variable Checkerspot, also known as the Chalcedon Checkerspot, is a medium-size butterfly with relatively narrow, pointed forewings and variable coloration depending on location. The upper surfaces of its wings are black to tawny brown and heavily checkered with white spots overall. Red to orange spots dot the wing margins and sometimes are seen in the forewing discal cell. The base of the leading edge of the forewing is also reddish. The wing undersides are also heavily spotted, but the background color is brownish orange. The body is black above with red-orange marks on its underside, white spots on the abdomen, and more orange-red marks on the palps. Yellow, bulbous clubs sit at the tips of the antennae. The caterpillar is black with white spots or stripes and is lined with fine, bristly spines that arise from orange bases. The caterpillar eats a variety of plants, including snapdragons, Indian paintbrush, penstemon, and monkey flower. Adults feed on flower nectar.

Rosy Maple Moth, *Dryocampa rubicunda*
Order: Lepidoptera (Butterflies and Moths)
Size: Wingspan 1¼–2"
Habitat: Deciduous woodlands
Range: Throughout eastern United States

The Rosy Maple Moth is a medium-size moth with a stocky, thick body. The upperside wings are simply patterned pink at the bases and margins, and are pale to bright yellow in between. The underside is patterned similarly but is paler overall. This moth usually holds its wings flat or arched up across the back like a tent. The hairy body is yellow above with pink patches below, is especially thick at the thorax, and has pink legs and broad, orange, feathered antennae. The light green caterpillar has tiny black dots, an orange-red head, and two black tubercules on the front end. The caterpillar eats leaves from a variety of broadleaf trees, including maple, oak, and beech. Adults do not feed.

Polyphemus Moth, *Antheraea polyphemus*
Order: Lepidoptera (Butterflies and Moths)
Size: Wingspan 3½–5¾"
Habitat: Deciduous woodlands, gardens
Range: Throughout the contiguous United States

The Polyphemus Moth, a very large, common silkmoth with a stout, heavily furred body, is named for the mythical Cyclops Polyphemus, who had a single eye. The upperside wings are light to dark brown overall. The forewing has a small, black-bordered, white discal eyespot; small black apical patches; a dark submarginal line; and a reddish basal stripe. The hindwing has very large black eyespots encircling yellow, and a broad, dark submarginal stripe. The underside is paler overall with only a suggestion of eyespots. The body is brownish overall, above and below, with feathered antennae that are more pronounced in the male. The caterpillar is bright green with a brown head, banded with thin yellow stripes and dotted with orange tubercules bearing thin, dark spines. The caterpillar eats leaves from a variety of broadleaf trees, including oak, willow, apple, hawthorn, and birch. Adults do not feed. The illustration shows the adult male.

Cecropia Moth, *Hyalophora cecropia*
Order: Lepidoptera (Butterflies and Moths)
Size: Wingspan 4–6"
Habitat: Open woodlands, gardens, orchards
Range: Throughout eastern United States and southeastern California

The Cecropia Moth is a huge silk moth—indeed the largest moth in North America—and is colored with a rich tapestry of reds, browns, and white. The upperside wings have a background color of charcoal brown and pale margins, with both wings showing red-and-white crescent-shaped spots toward their interiors. The forewing has a black eyespot at the apex. The underside is patterned similarly but is paler overall. The upper surface of the body is reddish brown on the thorax and striped white, red, and black on the abdomen; its underside is spotted below. The legs are orange-red, and there is a white collar behind the head. Females have a plump abdomen and thin antennae, while males have narrower abdomens and very bushy antennae. The caterpillar is plump and light green, and has orange tubercles on the head and back and rows of blue tubercles along the sides. The caterpillar eats leaves from a variety of broadleaf trees, including maple, birch, walnut, plum, and cherry. Adults do not feed.

Regal Moth, *Citheronia regalis*
Order: Lepidoptera (Butterflies and Moths)
Size: Wingspan 3½–6"
Habitat: Deciduous woodlands, gardens, parks
Range: Throughout eastern United States, especially in the southeastern region

The Regal Moth, also known as the Royal Walnut Moth, is a massive, large-bodied moth. The upperside wings have a gray-to-brown background color with scattered pale yellow spots on the inner portion; the margins are unmarked. The hindwing is paler and more orange, while the forewing has unusual red-orange veins. Females are larger than males. The body is well furred, thick, striped reddish and pale yellow on the thorax, and banded on the abdomen. The legs are red-orange, and the antennae are relatively small and feathery. The caterpillar, known as the "hickory horned devil," is very large and imposing, green, and marked with black spots and lines, and has several long, arching, red-orange horns on the head and thorax. The caterpillar eats leaves from a variety of trees from the walnut family (Juglandaceae), including hickory, walnut, sweet gum, and pecan. Adults do not feed.

Sheep Moth, *Hemileuca eglanterina*
Order: Lepidoptera (Butterflies and Moths)
Size: Wingspan 2–3"
Habitat: A variety of habitats including coastal areas, mountains, woodlands, pastures, and scrubland
Range: West of the Continental Divide in the contiguous United States, most especially in California and the northwestern states

The Sheep Moth, also known as the Elegant Sheep Moth, is a silk moth of the West that can be found flying during the day. The wing pattern and coloration are extremely variable. Generally, it is rosy to pink on the forewing and yellow-orange on the hindwing, with both wings showing large, central black spots, marginal streaks, and transverse bands. In some regions, however, the dark markings are more extensive, reduced, or entirely absent. The underside wings are patterned as above. The body is long for a silk moth, with a thin abdomen. It is yellow to pinkish with a black-banded abdomen and feathered antennae (broader in the male). The caterpillar is blackish, often with dorsal red spots and white lines along the sides, and has rows of highly branched orange and black spines. The caterpillar eats plants from the rose family (Roseaceae), ceanothus, willow, and aspen. Adults do not feed. The illustration shows the male.

White-lined Sphinx, *Hyles lineata*
Order: Lepidoptera (Butterflies and Moths)
Size: Wingspan 2½–3½"
Habitat: A variety of habitats including fields, gardens, and dry scrub
Range: Widespread throughout the contiguous United States

The White-lined Sphinx, worldwide in distribution, is sometimes referred to as the Striped Morning Sphinx because it flies during the day as well as at night. It is large bodied with a tapered abdomen and pointed, narrow wings. The upperside of the forewing is tan and dark brown with a broad pale stripe from the wing base to the tip, crossed by broad white veins. The hindwing is mostly pink with black at the base and just inside the outer margin. The underside wings are paler overall. The head and upper thorax of the body are brownish with white stripes, while the abdomen has black-and-white spotting along the top and sides. The antennae are long, with compact feathering. The caterpillar is plump, smooth, and blackish; shows variable amounts of yellow or green stripes and spots; and has a prominent, yellow-orange tail horn. The caterpillar eats a variety of plants, including apple, elm, evening primrose, and tomato. Adults feed on flower nectar, using their very long proboscises to probe deep into flowers.

Hummingbird Clearwing, *Hemaris thysbe*
Order: Lepidoptera (Butterflies and Moths)
Size: Wingspan 1½–2½"
Habitat: Gardens, meadows, roadsides
Range: From Alaska to Florida, most commonly in the eastern United States and rarely in the Southwest

The Hummingbird Clearwing is a common, medium-size hawk moth that is active during the day and resembles a small hummingbird with its rapid, hovering flight and compact body shape. The forewings are narrow and pointed, are reddish brown with olive green at the base, and have large, clear, scaleless patches along their central sections. The hindwings are much smaller and rounded, with similar clear patches. The body is robust, olive green above on the thorax and head, whitish below, with a dark reddish-brown to blackish abdomen that terminates in a broad tail tuft. The antennae are long, thick, and black. The caterpillar is fat and bright green, with longitudinal pale stripes and a single yellow to bluish tail horn. The caterpillar eats a variety of plants, including hawthorn, honeysuckle, cherry, plum, and snowberry. The adults feeds on flower nectar, using a long proboscis to probe deep into flowers.

Double-toothed Prominent, *Nerice bidentata*
Order: Lepidoptera (Butterflies and Moths)
Size: Wingspan 1¼–1½"
Habitat: Deciduous woodlands, parks, habitats where elm is found
Range: Throughout eastern United States

The Double-toothed Prominent is a small, common moth of the East with broad wings and scales at the basal edge of the fore-wings; these stand upright, hence the name "prominent." The upperside of the forewing is brown along the top half, grayish on the bottom half, with a ragged, dark, double-toothed edge in between. The hindwing is an unmarked brown, paler toward the base. With wings folded flat or angled as a tent, the moth appears convincingly as a strip of bark or dry leaves. The body is mottled pale gray-brown and has heavily furred legs and feathered anten-nae. The caterpillar, known as the "elm caterpillar," is small and green, with pale stripes above, yellow lines along the sides, and several raised, forked ridges along the back. The caterpillar eats the leaves of elms and related species.

Dogbane Tiger Moth, *Cycnia tenera*
Order: Lepidoptera (Butterflies and Moths)
Size: Wingspan 1¼–1¾"
Habitat: Meadows, roadsides, fields where dogbane is present
Range: Throughout the United States, most commonly in the eastern states

Also known as the Delicate Cycnia, the Dogbane Tiger Moth is a small to medium-size, ghostly, mostly nocturnal moth. It has the ability to communicate with other moths by echolocation, which is also thought to confuse bats who might prey on them. The upperside wings are pure white and nearly translucent, including the veins, except for a butter-yellow to golden strip along the leading edge of the forewing. The undersides are colored the same, with the addition of a dusky flush to the forewing just under the yellow strip. The head and sides of the thorax are bright yellow, the rest of the body is white, and there is a strip of black spots and yellow bands along the top and sides of the abdomen. The antennae are thin and lined black and white, as are the legs. The caterpillar is white to very pale brown or gray, and covered in long, soft hairs that arise from branching basal tufts. The caterpillar eats the leaves of the dogbane plant, milkweed, and Indian hemp.

Eight-spotted Forester, *Alypia octomaculata*
Order: Lepidoptera (Butterflies and Moths)
Size: Wingspan 1–1½"
Habitat: Open woodlands, fields, riparian areas, urban parks
Range: Throughout the United States, most commonly in the eastern states

The Eight-spotted Forester is a small, boldly patterned moth with strong flight that is active during the day. The upperside wings are rich black overall, with two large, pale yellow spots on the forewing and two large, white spots on the hindwing, although there may be variation in the number and size of these markings. The undersides of the wings are patterned as above. The body is black overall, with pale yellow sides to the thorax, variably occurring white spotting on top of the abdomen, bright orange tufts on the front two legs, and dark antennae that are thickened toward the tip but not noticeably feathered. The caterpillar is black with broad orange bands and thin, broken, white bands, and is spiked with thin pale hairs. The caterpillar eats a variety of plants, including grape, Virginia creeper, woodvine, and peppervine. Adults feed on flower nectar.

Garden Tiger Moth, *Arctia caja*
Order: Lepidoptera (Butterflies and Moths)
Size: Wingspan 2–2¾"
Habitat: A variety of habitats, especially damp areas, meadows, and streamsides
Range: Primarily the Pacific Northwest and Rocky Mountains, but also found in north-central and northeastern states

The Garden Tiger Moth is a beautiful, medium-size tiger moth with nocturnal habits and quite variable wing coloration. In general, the upperside of the forewing consists of a contrasting mosaic of reddish or dark brown patches over a white background. The hindwing is bright orange with large, black-rimmed blue spots and a pale margin. With the forewings folded down, the butterfly is camouflaged in grasses and brush, but when alarmed it flashes its brilliant hindwings to frighten predators. The body is dark brown above on the head and thorax, with a red collar at the neck, and is orange with broken, dark blue bands on the abdomen. It is mostly brownish orange below with pale, compact antennae. The caterpillar is of the "woolly bear" type, densely covered in long, pale-tipped black bristles with shorter reddish bristles near the base and at the neck. The caterpillar eats a wide variety of herbaceous and woody plants, including blackberry, clover, plum, plantain, birch, and apple.

Isabella Tiger Moth, *Pyrrharctia isabella*
Order: Lepidoptera (Butterflies and Moths)
Size: Wingspan 1¼–2½"
Habitat: Open deciduous woodlands, grasslands, gardens, parks
Range: Throughout the contiguous United States

The Isabella Tiger Moth is a common, medium-size moth, most often known by its larval form, the woolly bear caterpillar. The adult has relatively long, pointed forewings, which are colored light yellow-brown overall and sparsely marked with faint bars near the outer and medial sections. There are also variable numbers of small, dark spots on the interior and outer margin. The hindwing of the female is tinged orange to pink, whereas that of the male is pale yellow. The body is orange-brown with a hairy, tufted upper thorax; dark spots along the upper abdomen; thin, pale antennae; and black legs. The caterpillar is plump and covered with fuzzy, fine hairs. It is black with a wide, orange-brown central section. The caterpillar eats a wide variety of herbaceous and woody plants, including maples, clover, sunflowers, elm, and grasses.

Clymene, *Haploa clymene*
Order: Lepidoptera (Butterflies and Moths)
Size: Wingspan 1½–2"
Habitat: Deciduous woodlands, moist fields
Range: Eastern states, west to Texas and north to the Great Lakes

Named after the mythical Greek goddess of fame, the Clymene is an elegantly patterned, medium-size tiger moth that is active both day and night. The upperside of the forewing is bright to creamy white, with broad black marks near the leading edge and both outer and inner margins. With wings folded, the central black mark resembles a dagger. The hindwing is bright orange, yellow, or white, with a large dark spot near the lower margin (sometimes this is accompanied by an additional smaller spot). The underside is a relatively unpatterned rusty brown. The body is cream on the thorax and yellow-orange on the head and abdomen, with a dark dorsal stripe running the length of the body; it is uniformly reddish brown below. The antennae are long, black, and thin, and the legs are black. The caterpillar is mostly black, with sparse, fine, pale hairs and rows of yellow spots along the sides. The caterpillar eats the leaves of willow, oak, and plants in the sunflower family (Compositae).

Indian-Meal Moth, *Plodia interpunctella*
Order: Lepidoptera (Butterflies and Moths)
Size: Wingspan ½–¾"
Habitat: Indoor places with a food source, especially kitchens, pantries, and warehouses, or outside in warm climates (they do not tolerate cold)
Range: Worldwide

The Indian-Meal Moth is a native of South America that has become naturalized across the globe from the transport of foods that contain its eggs and larvae. It is also known as the Pantry Moth, and is a considerable pest in homes and anywhere dried foods are stored. The adult is tiny, with narrow forewings that are pale gray-brown at the base, dark reddish brown on the outer half, and overlaid with broad, broken, charcoal gray transverse bands. The hindwing is uniformly off-white, but is usually hidden by the tightly folded forewings. The surface of both wings may show a metallic sheen. The body is brown above, gray below, with long, thin antennae. The caterpillar, known as a "waxworm," is smooth and shiny, white, creamy, or pale gray, with a brown head. Feeding caterpillars will leave a residue of silk webbing inside the food source. The caterpillar eats various grains (especially cornmeal, from which its common name is derived), cereals, dried foods, and pet food. Adults do not feed.

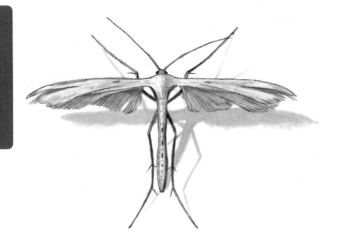

Morning Glory Plume Moth, *Emmelina monodactyla*
Order: Lepidoptera (Butterflies and Moths)
Size: Wingspan ¾–1"
Habitat: Fields and meadows where host plants are found
Range: Throughout the contiguous United States

The Morning Glory Plume Moth is a tiny moth that is active at dusk and has a highly modified body structure. The body is very long and narrow, with long, delicate legs that have thin, pointed spurs. The forewing is deeply cleft into two lobes, each with bristles near the tips. The hindwing is divided into three distinct plumes, each resembling a feather, with fine scales emanating from a central vein. The wings, which are commonly held tightly together and rolled up, appear as a solid stick. The rear legs are also often pressed against the body, giving rise to this moth's other common name, the T-Moth. The color overall is a light to dark brown, interrupted on top of the abdomen with a pale line that may be streaked with darker marks. The caterpillar is pale yellow-green with a broad, dark green stripe down the back, and is covered with fine, pale hairs. The caterpillar eats a variety of herbaceous plants, including bindweeds and morning glories (Convolvulaceae), lamb's quarters, and members of the nightshade family (Solanaceae).

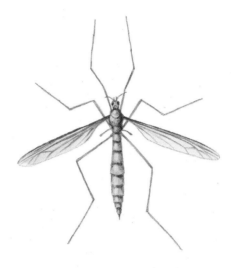

Crane Flies, *Tipula* spp.
Order: Diptera (Flies)
Size: Up to 1"
Habitat: Varied habitats, usually near water or moist soils; gardens, fields, indoors
Range: Throughout North America

Crane flies appear like giant mosquitoes, but are completely harmless. Many species inhabit North America, all of which have extremely long, thin legs (easily broken off); a long, thin abdomen; a broad thorax; long antennae; and one pair of thin wings. In place of rear wings, there is a pair of small projections that aid in balance. The color is drab gray or brownish. Females are sometimes wingless and have a thin, egg-laying projection (the ovipositor) at the rear (this is not a stinger, as some might fear). The larvae are grub-like with a tough, leathery skin, and feed on decaying plant matter and fungi, although some are pests of garden and crop plants. Adults rarely feed and commonly come indoors, where they lazily cling to curtains or window sidings.

Deer Flies, *Chrysops* spp.
Order: Diptera (Flies)
Size: Up to ½"
Habitat: Most environments near a water source; woodlands, meadows
Range: Throughout North America

Deer flies are closely related to the horse flies but are generally smaller. They are best known for the feeding habits of the females, who make a painful incision on the skin and suck out blood. Males feed on flower nectar. Both sexes have compact bodies about the same size or smaller than common house flies, wings with bold black markings, and bodies that are vividly patterned with stripes of black and gold. They lay a mass of black eggs on vegetation above water that hatch to whitish aquatic larvae. Although most common near water, adults may stray miles into nearby woodlands.

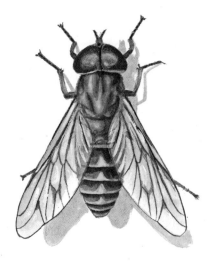

Horse Flies, *Tabanus* spp.
Order: Diptera (Flies)
Size: Up to 1"
Habitat: Most habitats near a water source; woodlands, marshes
Range: Throughout North America

Horse flies are related to the deer flies but are generally much larger. Their feeding habits are similar, however, slicing a small incision into the host and sucking out the blood, and they can be a serious pest to livestock. The body is robust with broad, black and green eyes and short, amber-colored, hornlike antennae. The thorax and abdomen are grayish to brownish, with weakly patterned paler areas at each abdominal segment. The wings are mostly clear with dark veins. An egg mass is laid on surfaces above water or on a moist substrate, and larvae feed on larval insects or worms in the soil. Adults are active during the day in the late summer months, and will live for only a matter of days.

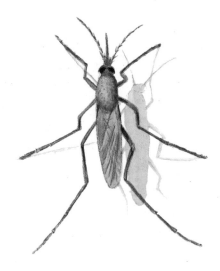

Mosquitoes (many species)
Order: Diptera (Flies)
Size: Up to ¼"
Habitat: Nearly all habitats close to a water source
Range: Throughout North America

Well-known to everyone, mosquitoes are a large group of delicate flies with thousands of known species. In general, they have small, elongate bodies; long, thin legs; thin wings with small scales; and a long, sharp proboscis. Females have feathery, plume-like antennae, while males have narrower, bristled antennae. Females feed on the blood of vertebrates, including humans, by secreting a saliva (which is responsible for causing itching) and sucking blood through the proboscis. Males feed on nectar and plant juices. Eggs are laid on the surface of any body of stagnant water, and the larvae, called "wrigglers," float on the water and breathe air through a small tube. These morph into another stage, the pupa, which does not feed. Adults are most active during twilight hours or at night. They are major vectors of disease such as malaria and yellow fever. The male of the *Aedes* genus is illustrated.

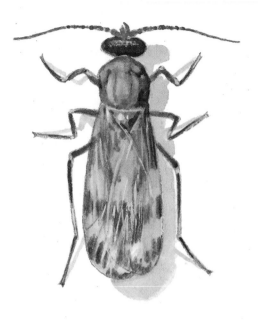

Biting Midges, *Culicoides* spp.
Order: Diptera (Flies)
Size: Up to ⅛"
Habitat: Wetlands, ponds, streams
Range: Throughout North America

Also known as "punkies" or "no-see-ums" because of their tiny size, biting midges gather in swarms and annoy campers and anglers with their cumulative, irritating bites. Unlike true midges, they hold their wings across the back instead of outstretched when at rest. The body resembles a small, compact mosquito, with a bulbous abdomen that swells during feeding and a small head that is positioned lower than the thorax. They are colored grayish to pale green, with light and dark patterned wings. The larvae are pale and wormlike, and live in or near water or other moist environments. Adults feed on nectar or vertebrate blood, or attack other insects.

Dog Flea, *Ctenocephalides canis*
Order: Siphonaptera (Fleas)
Size: Up to ⅟₁₆"
Habitat: On or near domestic dogs and cats
Range: Throughout North America

The Dog Flea is one of several similar fleas that host on a variety of mammals and birds. These insects are parasites mainly on dogs, but will use cats as a host as well, and will also bite humans. The body is tiny, wingless, hardened, and flattened vertically, which enables it to pass easily through animal hairs. They have an amazing ability to jump (up to a foot high), aided by strong inner leg segments and long rear legs. The mouthparts are specially adapted to pierce and suck the blood of its host. The color is light to dark brown. Backward-facing bristles on the body enable them to cling to hairs, making it difficult to remove them by scratching. Eggs are laid either on the host or on the ground, but the young always end up developing off the host, where they can survive for weeks without feeding.

Little Black Ant, *Monomorium minimum*
Order: Hymenoptera (Ants, Bees, and Wasps)
Size: Up to ⅟₁₆"
Habitat: Woodlands, rural areas, houses
Range: Throughout North America

Little Black Ants are common, tiny ants that are probably best known for finding their way into kitchens or pantries in search of food scraps. They have a complex social structure, with a queen (or queens) that produces eggs and workers that tend to the young and collect food for the colony. Workers are shiny black or dark brown and wingless, with elbowed antennae. The narrow waist, or pedicel, has two segments (although you'll need a magnifying glass to see this). When a worker ant locates food, it communicates its find to other ants, and soon a trail of workers is formed from the food source to the colony. Colonies are located underground, in rotting woodpiles, or in voids in foundations and patios. The small size of these ants allows them to move through even the narrowest cracks in walls and flooring.

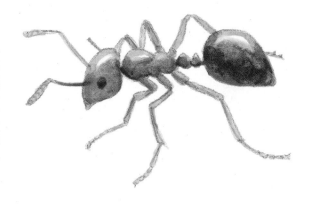

Fire Ant, *Solenopsis geminata*
Order: Hymenoptera (Ants, Bees, and Wasps)
Size: Up to ¼"
Habitat: Woodlands and open spaces, usually sunny areas near a water source
Range: Throughout the United States, mostly in southern latitudes

Fire Ants are known for the painful sting they can inflict, which produces a burning sensation. They are highly social, and a colony includes queens, mating males, soldiers, and workers. The most prevalent caste is the workers, who collect all kinds of plant material and insects. They are fairly small, with typical ant features such as a bulbous head and abdomen, thin legs, elbowed antennae, and a thin waist area (pedicel) with two segments. They are colored bronze to reddish brown, with a darker abdomen that ends in a stinger. Soldiers also possess enlarged pincers for defense. Fire Ants form large colonies on the ground, under logs or rocks, or in a self-created dirt mound. The worker ant is illustrated.

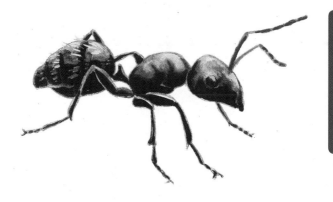

Black Carpenter Ant, *Camponotus pennsylvanicus*
Order: Hymenoptera (Ants, Bees, and Wasps)
Size: Up to ⅝"
Habitat: Deciduous woodlands, logs, fields, wooden structures
Range: Central and eastern United States

Black Carpenter Ants are large ants that form complex colonies in some form of wood source, although they do not eat the wood, but chew it away for nesting cavities. Colonies consist of different types of these ants, including a queen and different-size workers. In general, they have the familiar ant-like constricted waist region and clearly elbowed antennae. They are colored jet black and have yellowish hairs on the abdomen. They feed on just about anything, including a wide variety of insects, aphid honeydew, fungi, fruits, and scraps from humans (especially sweets). A scout ant, upon finding a food source, leaves a chemical trail back to the nest to notify others where to go. It is best not to handle these ants, as they can deliver a painful bite.

Bumble Bees, *Bombus spp*

Order: Hymenoptera (Ants, Bees, and Wasps)
Size: Up to ¾"
Habitat: Open woodlands, gardens, fields
Range: Throughout most of the United States, especially northern latitudes

Bumble bees are easily recognized by their large, robust bodies, which are covered in long, fine hairs, and their lazy "bumbling" flight. Like ants and wasps, they have a very thin waist (pedicel), but it is obscured by hair, giving them a plump look. The color is yellow overall except for a black head and a black band between the wings. Female workers have specialized rear legs with a shiny, concave basket for transporting pollen. Bumble bees are extremely important ecologically as pollinators of a wide variety of flowering plants. Worker bees forage away from the nest (which is placed on the ground or in a depression), where they drink flower nectar for energy and collect pollen that is made into honey to feed the young. They are not aggressive, and although they can sting, they rarely do except as a last resort in self-defense.

Honey Bees, *Apis spp*
Order: Hymenoptera (Ants, Bees, and Wasps)
Size: Up to ⅝"
Habitat: Open woodlands, fields, orchards, gardens
Range: Throughout North America

Native to Europe, honey bees were introduced to North America in the 1800s and are now well established around the world. They are extremely important as pollinators of all kinds of flowering plants and commercial crops, and for their production of honey and wax. Their hives are located in hollow trees or man-made boxes, where there is a complex social structure of queens, domestic males (drones), and thousands of worker females. They all have two sets of membranous wings, a very thin waist region, and elbowed antennae. The color is reddish brown with distinctive yellow and black bands on the nearly hairless abdomen. Workers use specialized rear legs with a "basket" to transport pollen and a crop to store nectar, both of which help to feed the colony. These bees can deliver a painful sting if threatened, and a barb on the stinger causes it to lodge into its victim and ultimately kill the bee.

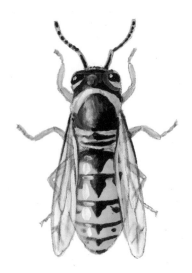

Western Yellowjacket, *Vespula pensylvanica*
Order: Hymenoptera (Ants, bees, and wasps)
Size: Up to ½"
Habitat: Fields, woodland edges, rural yards
Range: Western half of North America

Yellowjackets are a kind of wasp, in a different group than the hairy, pollen-collecting bees (even though they are sometimes called "meat bees"). The Western Yellowjacket has a stout, smooth body with two pairs of grayish transparent wings, and a distinct black-and-yellow banded abdomen. They are scavengers for all types of food, including meat, and eat a variety of insects, slugs, and nectar. They form colonies centered about a chambered, papery nest found on buildings, on trees, or in the ground, made of digested wood pulp. New nests are built each year. Females are capable of stinging multiple times and are easily provoked. Bites are not serious unless the victim has an allergy to the venom. They are nearly identical to the Eastern Yellowjacket of the eastern United States.

ARACHNIDS

Black Widow, *Latrodectus mactans*
Order: Araneae (Spiders)
Size: Up to ⅜" (females larger than males)
Habitat: Dark, hidden areas in woodpiles, sheds, debris, etc.
Range: Throughout the United States

The Black Widow is one of the most feared spiders due to its secretive but dangerous nature, and although its bite is rarely fatal, it can cause serious illness. The female is glossy black with a large, rounded abdomen, medium-length legs, and a bright red, hourglass-shaped spot on the underside (this may appear as two separate red lines divided by black). The male has a much smaller body but with relatively long legs, and is paler in color with dull reddish marks on the abdomen. Both sexes are capable of injecting venom, but the female gives a larger volume. They feed on insects or other spiders that become ensnared in their webs, whereby they wrap the prey in silk and ingest the juices. Commonly, the female will eat the male after mating. The underside of the female is illustrated.

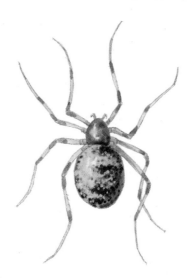

American House Spider, *Parasteatoda tepidariorum*
Order: Araneae (Spiders)
Size: Up to ¼" (females larger than males)
Habitat: Houses, barns, sheds, and other buildings
Range: Throughout the United States

This common spider is a member of the group known as "cobweb weavers" or "combfooted spiders" because of the irregular webs they weave and the presence of comblike bristles on the end of the hind legs. As with most spiders, there is a small cephalothorax (head and thorax combined) that bears four pairs of walking legs, and a larger, bulbous abdomen (especially large in females). There are no antennae, and the mouthparts are flanked by a pair of small, sharp fangs. The color is light brown with variable blackish and gray patches and mottling on the abdomen. When prey is trapped in the web, this spider will encase it with extra silk and often carry it to another location to suck out the fluids. It generally avoids humans and runs away or feigns death if disturbed, but rough handling could result in a minor but painful bite. The female is illustrated.

Banded Garden Spider, *Argiope trifasciata*
Order: Araneae (Spiders)
Size: Up to 1" (females larger than males)
Habitat: Gardens, grassy fields, thickets
Range: Throughout the United States

Also known as the Banded Argiope, this spider is in the group known as the "orb-weavers" because their webs are composed of round, spiraling rings of silk suspended between grasses and shrubs. The abdomen is elongate and pointy at the rear. The legs are fairly long and, when at rest, are held with the front two pairs forward and the back two pairs behind. Females have a creamy or yellow abdomen with thin black bands and a fuzzy, grayish carapace. Males are substantially smaller than females and have a pale gray, gold-speckled abdomen. The web is up to 2 feet across, built in the early morning and subsequently eaten at the close of day. A new web will be made the next morning. The spider waits in the center of its web, head down, for any insects flying or jumping into it, whereby it wraps the prey in silk and sucks out the juices. It can deliver a bite if harassed or if it senses that its eggs are in danger. The female is illustrated.

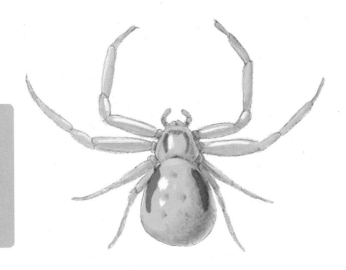

Goldenrod Crab Spider, *Misumena vatia*
Order: Araneae (Spiders)
Size: Up to ⅜" (females larger than males)
Habitat: Areas with flowering plants; gardens, fields
Range: Throughout the United States

The Goldenrod Crab Spider is a member of the group known as "crab spiders" because they typically hold their legs out to the sides of the body, like crabs, and prefer to crawl sideways more than forward or backward. The first two pairs of legs are noticeably longer than the hind two, and are held out for grasping prey. The color of the body can change to match the surroundings, from whitish to bright yellow (like the goldenrod flower), and there are usually red marks on either side of the abdomen and between the eyes. The male is smaller than the female, with a small abdomen but proportionately longer legs, and has a brownish body with a pale spot on the center of the carapace. This species is considered a "flower spider," those that do not spin a web but climb onto plants and flowers waiting to ambush visiting insects (especially pollinators). They are harmless to humans. The female is illustrated.

Carolina Wolf Spider, *Hogna carolinensis*
Order: Araneae (Spiders)
Size: Up to 1" (females larger than males)
Habitat: Drier areas of woodlands, grasslands, deserts
Range: Throughout the United States

The wolf spiders are a fairly common group of ground-dwelling or burrowing spiders with hairy bodies, long and stout legs, and excellent eyesight. The abdomen and cephalothorax are about the same size. The Carolina Wolf Spider is the largest wolf spider in the United States. Its color is cryptic and often matches the habitat, usually pale brown or gray with a dark mark on the top side of the abdomen. They are solid black underneath, and may have orange pedipalps (mouthparts). This spider excavates burrows to 6 inches deep as a retreat, and ventures out at night to feed on insects or even small mammals. The tiny young, after hatching, cling to the mother's back until they are old enough to fend for themselves.

Bold Jumping Spider, *Phidippus audax*
Order: Araneae (Spiders)
Size: Up to ⅝"
Habitat: Gardens, fields, open woodlands
Range: Throughout the United States

The jumping spiders are a group of small, hairy, compact, short-legged spiders with an incredible jumping ability. They also have four pairs of eyes, two of which are large and forward facing, giving them highly developed stereo vision. The Bold Jumping Spider is quite large for a jumping spider, and is colored mostly black with scattered white and gray markings (juveniles have orange on the abdomen). The chelicerae (front fangs) are iridescent bluish green. These spiders are active during the day, especially in bright light, when they can use their keen vision to locate prey. They set a silken tagline and leap at their victims, even those in flight. If the spider misses the target, it can climb its way back via the tagline. Insects and other spiders are eaten, even those much larger in size than itself.

California Trapdoor Spider, *Bothriocyrtum californicum*
Order: Araneae (Spiders)
Size: Up to 1¼"
Habitat: Sunny areas of firm soil, including steep banks
Range: Southern California

The trapdoor spiders are unique in that they construct a neat, silk-lined burrow with a thin, hinged lid that, when closed, is nearly impossible to detect. Here the spider waits for the passage of nearby prey, then leaps out of the hole to attack. The meal is then dragged into the burrow, up to 8 inches deep, where it is eaten. The California Trapdoor Spider is fairly large, with a flattened, wide cephalothorax, a bulbous abdomen, and thick, stubby legs. The fangs are robust and serrated to help in burrow excavation. The body is hairless and shiny, black on the legs and cephalothorax, and grayish or light reddish brown on the abdomen. Males are smaller than females but have proportionately larger, thinner legs. The female is illustrated.

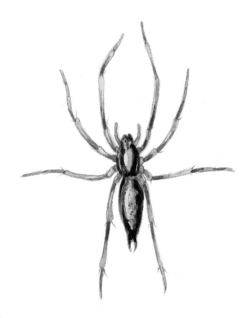

Grass Spiders, *Agelenopsis* spp.
Order: Araneae (Spiders)
Size: Up to ¾"
Habitat: Gardens, grassy fields
Range: Throughout the United States

The grass spider, several species of which exist in North America, is a member of the group known as "tunnel weavers," who weave a flat web in grasses with a funnel-shaped section to one side, where the spider waits for prey. When a prey insect ensnares in the web, the spider scurries out to inject it with venom and carries it back into the funnel section to feed. Grass spiders are cryptically colored in browns and grays, with a light tan cephalothorax that has two darker brown stripes, and a mottled gray, teardrop-shaped abdomen, which terminates in pointed spinerettes (the silk-producing organs). The legs are long and thin. Grass spiders are harmless to humans, being shy and retreating to safety when encountered.

Desert Tarantula, *Aphonopelma chalcodes*
Order: Araneae (Spiders)
Size: Up to 2½"
Habitat: Deserts
Range: Southwestern United States

Desert Tarantulas are large, fearsome-looking spiders, covered
in long, dense hairs, that live in the extreme heat and dryness
of deserts of Arizona, New Mexico, and Southern California. The
females are light brown overall, while the males are dark brown
on the abdomen and have black leg bases. During the day they
keep under rocks or use burrows made by rodents. They emerge
at night to hunt for a variety of insects or small lizards, which they
subdue with large fangs and mild venom. Although feared by
many, bites are not more serious than a common bee sting, and
bristly hairs on the abdomen can break off and cause skin irritation. Female desert tarantulas can live for up to twenty years, and
are sometimes kept as pets. The male is illustrated.

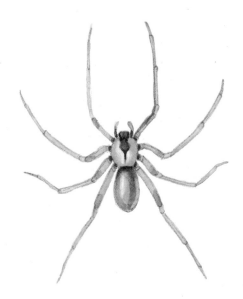

Brown Recluse, *Loxosceles reclusa*
Order: Araneae (Spiders)
Size: Up to ½"
Habitat: Houses, barns, outside under debris or rocks
Range: South-central United States

The Brown Recluse is a small brown spider with long, spindly legs. It is sometimes called a "violin spider" because of the violin-shaped dark mark on the cephalothorax. Otherwise, it is some shade of yellowish or reddish brown, sometimes with a darker abdomen. These spiders are most active at night, hunting small insects or finding prey trapped in their loose, unorganized webs in sheltered places. They are rather reclusive (as the common name suggests) and will avoid people and usually run away in defense. However, this is a potentially dangerous spider because of its powerful venom, and because it often hides in closets or on clothing and towels. If bitten, the wound is painful and deep, and may take months to heal. In severe cases a bite can be fatal.

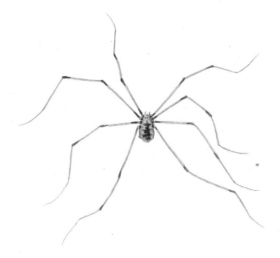

Striped Daddy Long legs, *Leiobunum vittatum*
Order: Opiliones (Harvestmen)
Size: Up to ¼"
Habitat: Woodlands, gardens, shrubbery
Range: Central and eastern United States

These curious arachnids are not true spiders, but belong to a group known as harvestman spiders. Many species occur in North America, and most have a distinctive oval, flattened body with a broadly fused head, thorax, and abdomen, and extremely long, thin legs. Despite the long legs, they are held bent and the body stays close to the ground. Like spiders, they have eight legs, but the second pair is longer than the others and is often used in sensory perception. The Striped Daddy Long legs has a pale body with dark stripes down the back and blackish legs. It feeds on decaying plant material or small insects, and will often congregate in clusters on the warm sides of buildings or tree trunks. Contrary to some myths, harvestmen have very small feeding pincers, are nonvenomous, and are completely harmless to humans. They easily break off a leg in self-defense that will not regenerate.

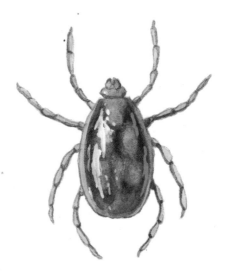

Brown Dog Tick, *Rhipicephalus sanguineus*
Order: Parasitiformes (Ticks)
Size: ⅛" or larger
Habitat: Yards, homes, on dogs or other mammals
Range: Throughout North America

Ticks are considered a kind of large mite, and as such are related to the spiders (not insects). They have a tear-shaped body with no segmentation, eight legs of uniform length, piercing mouthparts, and no antennae. The abdomen is capable of enlarging greatly when engorged with blood to become many times the normal size. They are uniformly reddish brown. Dog ticks feed by creating a small incision through which they suck blood from the host animal, particularly a dog, but other mammals may also serve as hosts. This tick can undergo an entire life cycle indoors, unlike other ticks that must spend at least a portion of their lives out of doors. Throughout the life stages from egg to larvae to nymph to adult, it may transfer to as many as three different hosts, and females lay clumps of thousands of tiny eggs. Although these ticks cause irritation and itching in dogs, they are relatively harmless to humans.

Red Velvet Mite, *Trombidium holosericeum*
Order: Trombidiformes (Mites)
Size: Up to ⅛"
Habitat: Moist woodlands, gardens
Range: Throughout North America

Mites are arachnids, the same group as spiders, and as such they have eight legs. They are generally quite small, with a globular, undivided, expandable body; piercing and sucking mouthparts; and no antennae. The Red Velvet Mite is aptly named, as the body and legs are bright red-orange and covered with fine, velvety hairs. The tiny red larvae of this species attach to an insect host to feed on body fluids, but adults roam free and eat small invertebrates, larvae, and eggs. Although many species of mites are harmful for the diseases they transmit, the Red Velvet Mite is completely harmless to humans.

Mordant Scorpion, *Uroctonus mordax*
Order: Scorpiones (Scorpions)
Size: Up to 2½"
Habitat: Moist forested areas
Range: California and Oregon

Scorpions are in the same class as spiders (the arachnids) but belong to their own order (Scorpiones). As a group, they have elongate, segmented bodies; eight legs; conspicuous pincers; and a long, thin tail that is held arced over the body and ends in a stinger. The color is reddish brown or yellowish. Although fearsome looking, the Mordant Scorpion is relatively harmless to humans and is sometimes kept as a pet. The sting can be painful but is not poisonous to humans. At night, they reside in underground burrows, under rocks, or around decaying logs, emerging during the day to feed on insects and spiders. The pincers are used to grab prey and bring it to the mouthparts, while the stinger is used mainly for defense. Females birth up to three dozen tiny young that cling to her back until they are able to fend for themselves.

CRUSTACEANS

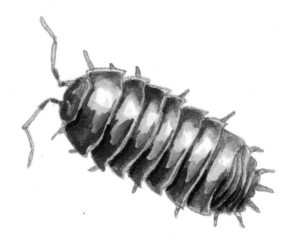

Sowbugs (many species)
Order: Isopoda (Sowbugs and Allies)
Size: Up to ½"
Habitat: Gardens, woodlands; moist places under rocks and logs
Range: Throughout the United States

The large group of invertebrates that includes sowbugs (also known as "woodlice") are not insects but crustaceans, being related to the crabs and lobsters. They are small and oblong, with a flattened carapace composed of several segments. They have seven pairs of legs of nearly equal length; tiny, simple eyes; and two taillike projections (uropods). Their color is some shade of gray or brown. Some species can roll their bodies into a tight ball and are known as "pill bugs" or "roly-polies." Sowbugs stay in secluded, dark, damp places during the day and venture out at night to feed on plants, leaves, and decaying organic matter with chewing mouthparts. The eggs are carried in brood pouches on the underside of females and hatch to young that look like miniature adults.

Pacific Mole Crab, *Emerita analoga*
Order: Decapoda (Mole Crabs or Sand Crabs)
Size: Up to 1½" (females larger than males)
Habitat: Intertidal zone on sandy beaches
Range: Coastal western United States

The ubiquitous Pacific Mole Crab (also known as the Pacific Sand Crab) thrives on sandy beaches in the zone where the waves wash in and out. Facing the water, they plant their hindquarters in the sand, and as a wave retreats, they use specialized antennae to filter tiny bits of planktonic material into their mouths. When uncovered by water, they quickly burrow backward into the sand to avoid predation by hungry shorebirds. The sand crab's body is compact and sturdy, with a tough, sand-colored carapace to protect its thin legs, eyes, and antennae. The tail can be brought up under the body for further protection. Females are typically larger than males, and can be identified by clusters of bright orange eggs on their undersides. Shore anglers are fond of these crabs as bait, as they are a favored prey of many fish.

GASTROPODS

Garden Snail, *Helix aspersa*
Class: Gastropoda (Snails and Slugs)
Size: Shell 1¼" diameter
Habitat: Shady or moist areas, gardens, croplands
Range: Throughout North America

Garden Snails were introduced from Europe and are now widespread in North America. This is the snail you are most likely to see in your garden. The body is like a gray slug with a thin, spiraled, brown shell with darker brown or black bands and striations. When active, the long foot, head, and two sets of tentacles are extended, but the soft parts will quickly retract into the shell if threatened. During very dry weather they can survive by contracting into the shell and sealing the bottom with mucus. They are mostly active at night or during the day during wet weather, feeding on a wide variety of plants with a rasping tongue. Though not the typical snail used as escargot in cuisine, it is still edible and considered a delicacy by some.

Banana Slugs, *Ariolimax* spp.
Class: Gastropoda (Snails and Slugs)
Size: Up to 10"
Habitat: Moist forests
Range: Pacific states, California to Alaska

The banana slug is the largest slug in North America, with three species represented along the humid forests of the Pacific Northwest and California. They are conspicuous by their size and their bright yellow coloring, although they are occasionally brown, whitish, or spotted. As a group, the slugs are snails without shells (or with small remnants of a shell) that have a long, muscular foot for locomotion, two sets of antennae, and a hole on the right side of the body for respiration. The slime on the exterior acts as protection from desiccation and as a deterrent to predators. Banana slugs feed on dead leaves and other plant matter, fungi, and feces with rasping mouthparts. They are hermaphrodites, meaning that each slug possesses both male and female reproductive organs, although two slugs usually come together to mate, after which eggs are laid in leaf litter. The Pacific Banana Slug is illustrated.

Leopard Slug, *Limax maximus*
Class: Gastropoda (Snails and Slugs)
Size: Up to 6"
Habitat: Woodlands, gardens, urban areas
Range: Throughout North America

Also known as the "spotted garden slug," this species is indigenous to Europe but is now common and widespread in North America, and is the slug you are most likely to see under rocks and scraps of wood in your backyard. The body is grayish or brown with black "leopard spots" on the mantle and broken black lines along the sides and lower back. There is a long, muscular foot and two sets of retractable tentacles on the head for smelling and light detection. The posterior of the body is wrinkled and slightly keeled. Leopard Slugs feed on plants, decaying organic material, and mushrooms, and are sometimes pests in gardens. They lay a mass of clear, round eggs that develop directly into small slugs. Active at night, they will become dormant in times of dry weather.

SNAILS AND SLUGS

Meadow Slug, *Deroceras laeve*
Class: Gastropoda (Snails and Slugs)
Size: Up to 1"
Habitat: Marshes, moist woodlands, rural areas
Range: Throughout North America

Also known as the "marsh slug" or "brown slug," this is an introduced species from the Old World that is now common and widespread in North America. It is quite small and nondescript, about
as long as a quarter, with a cylindrical body, a tapered tail end,
and an elongate oval mantle. There are subtle, concentric ridges
on the front half of the back and two pairs of dark gray, stubby
tentacles. The color can be tan, brown, blackish, or a mottled com-
bination of these, and the skin is somewhat translucent. The foot,
on the underside, is thin and whitish. Meadow Slugs are relatively
active, feed on plants or decaying organic material, and can be
pests in gardens or greenhouses. They flourish in very moist areas,
can survive periods being submerged in water, and can even tolerate freezing temperatures.

Black Slug, *Arion ater*
Class: Gastropoda (Snails and Slugs)
Size: Up to 6"
Habitat: Moist fields, gardens
Range: Pacific Northwest region

The Black Slug is a large slug introduced from Europe and is now common in the northwestern United States. The body is elongate and broad, with a rounded back and blunt tail section. The front half of the body is topped by a raised mantle covered in small tubercles, while the back half has long, linear ridges. As with other slugs, it has a pair of long, light-sensing tentacles; a pair of shorter, smelling tentacles; and a tough foot running the length of its underside for locomotion. The color of the mucous-covered skin is generally jet black, but variants may be whitish or brownish. Young slugs are colored tan or reddish but attain darker colors with maturity. Black Slugs are active mostly during the wetness and coolness of night, feeding on plants, fungi, and decaying organic matter, and can be a pest of crops and gardens.

ANNELIDS

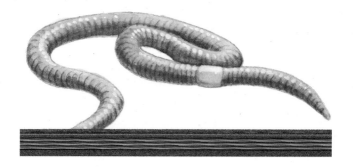

Earthworms (many species)
Class: Oligochaeta (Earthworms)
Size: ½–14"
Habitat: Moist soils and compost; under logs and rocks
Range: Throughout North America

The class of earthworms consists of well over a thousand species, but they all share a similar body plan even if their size varies considerably. Essentially, they are like segmented tubes, tapered at both ends, with a mucus-covered skin (cuticle) and very simple internal organs and sensory apparatus. They make tunnels through soil by pushing aside the soil or by ingesting it and expelling the remains behind (one can see little piles of these remains, called castings, near a tunnel entrance). For grip, they are lined with tiny, tough bristles that stick to the soil, and wavelike contractions move the body forward. They are all very beneficial to soil health by increasing aeration and releasing partially digested organic matter that plant roots easily absorb. Earthworms reproduce by coupling together at an enlarged band (the clitellum) and produce small egg capsules. The Red Wriggler, *Eisenia fetida*, is illustrated.

EARTHWORMS

Freshwater Leech, *Macrobdella decora*
Class: Clitellata (Leeches)
Size: Up to 2"
Habitat: Freshwater lakes, stagnant streams
Range: Northern regions of the United States

Leeches are segmented worms related to earthworms, but they have solid bodies, no external bristles, and suckers on both ends of the body. Some are terrestrial, but the most common forms in North America are aquatic and lurk in shallow, slow-moving fresh waters. They either swim about or move like inchworms on the bottoms, alternately attaching and releasing their suckers. The Freshwater Leech is brown or olive green with black and red spotting, and is banded with thin grooves. To feed, it attaches to a vertebrate host (including humans), makes a small incision, and sucks out blood. Anticoagulants in the saliva may cause the wound to bleed even after the leech has detached. Leeches have been used historically as an aid to bloodletting, and in modern medicine they are sometimes used to help relieve fluid pressure.

MYRIAPODS

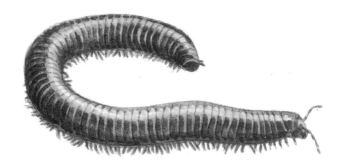

Millipedes (many species)
Class: Diplopoda (Millipedes)
Size: Up to 4"
Habitat: Under rocks and logs around moist soils and leaf litter
Range: Throughout North America

The familiar and friendly millipedes are part of a group of inverte-brates known as myriapods, which also includes the centipedes. They have long, cylindrical or flattened bodies with many hard-ened, thin segments, most of which bear two pairs of tiny legs. The word *millipede* means "thousand legs," and although this is an exaggeration, species with over a hundred legs are not uncom-mon (the record is 752 legs!). After hatching, most millipedes have only three pairs of legs, and with each molt more legs are added. They are relatively slow moving on land, and mostly bur-row through soil headed by a tough shield behind the head and propelled by the force of their many legs. Millipedes feed on decaying organic matter and plants, and are important for the health of soils, like earthworms. They do not bite or sting, and thus are completely harmless to humans. In defense, they crawl away, twist into a compact spiral, or roll into a ball like a pill bug. The American Giant Millipede, *Narceus americanus*, is illustrated.

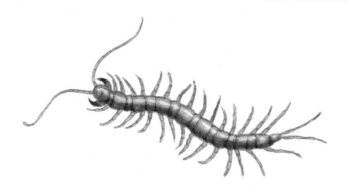

Centipedes (many species)
Class: Chilopoda (Centipedes)
Size: Up to 1¾"
Habitat: Under rocks and logs around moist soils and leaf litter
Range: Throughout North America

Centipedes are in the same group (myriapods) as millipedes, but they have only one pair of legs for each body segment (millipedes have two pairs per segment). The name *centipede* means "hundred legs," but in actuality the amount can vary from just over a dozen to well over a hundred. The body is highly segmented and flattened, allowing them great mobility and the ability to squeeze into tight areas. They run quite fast and use their tactile antennae as the key method of perception. Centipedes are very sensitive to desiccation, so they are restricted to moist areas and are normally active at night. They are predators on other invertebrates, including insects, spiders, slugs, and worms, which they seize with venom-laced claws near the head. If handled roughly, they can give a painful but nonserious bite. The Stone Centipede, *Lithobius forficatus*, is illustrated.

Bugs and Slugs by Region

Throughout the United States

American Cockroach
American House Spider
Banded Garden Spider
Black Swallowtail
Black Widow
Bold Jumping Spider
Boxelder Bug
Brown Dog Tick
Buckeye
Cabbage Butterfly
Carolina Wolf Spider
Common Black Ground Beetle
Eight-spotted Forester
European Earwig
Fire Ant
Goldenrod Crab Spider
Grass Spiders
Gray Hairstreak
Green Darner
Green Stink Bug
Harlequin Bug
Indian-Meal Moth
Isabella Tiger Moth
Monarch
Morning Glory Plume Moth
Mourning Cloak
Orange Sulfur
Painted Lady
Pipevine Swallowtail
Polyphemus Moth
Red Admiral

Red Velvet Mite
Southern Dogface
Sowbugs
Three-lined Potato Beetle
Violet Tail
White-lined Sphinx

Western United States
Banana Slugs
Blue-eyed Darner
Garden Tiger Moth
Jerusalem Cricket
Mordant Scorpion
Pacific Coast Termite
Pacific Mole Crab
Sheep Moth
Ten-lined June Beetle
Variable Checkerspot
Variegated Meadowhawk

Eastern United States
American Copper
Black Carpenter Ant
Cecropia Moth
Clymene
Convergent Ladybird Beetle
Dogbane Tiger Moth
Double-toothed Prominent
Eastern Tiger Swallowtail
Eight-spotted Forester
Eyed Click Beetle
Hummingbird Clearwing
Northern Walkingstick
Praying Mantis
Pyralis Firefly

Reddish-brown Stag Beetle
Red-spotted Purple
Regal Moth
Rosy Maple Moth
Striped Daddy Long-legs

Central United States

Northern Walkingstick
Grand Western Cicada
American Copper
Clymene
Pyralis Firefly
Garden Tiger Moth
Black Carpenter Ant
Brown Recluse
Striped Daddy Long-legs

Southern United States

Buckeye
Fire Ant
Pipevine Swallowtail
Southern Dogface

Southwestern United States

California Trapdoor Spider
Cecropia Moth
Desert Tarantula
Grand Western Cicada

Southeastern United States

Brown Recluse
Eastern Lubber Grasshopper
Regal Moth
Sweet Potato Weevil

Northern United States

American Cooper
Biting Midges
Brown Dog Tick
Bumble Bees
Cave Cricket
Centipedes
Common Black Ground Beetle
Crane Flies
Deer Flies
Dog Flea
Earthworms
European Earwig
Field Crickets
Fork-tailed Bush Katydid
Freshwater Leech
Garden Snail
Green Lacewings
Green Peach Aphid
Honey Bees
Horse Flies
Leopard Slug
Little Black Ant
Mayflies
Meadow Slug
Millipedes
Mosquitoes
Red Velvet Mite
Springtails
Three-lined Potato Beetle
Western Yellowjacket

Northwestern United States

Banana Slug
Black Slug

Garden Tiger Moth
Mordant Scorpion
Pacific Mole Crab
Praying Mantis
Sheep Moth

Northeastern United States
Garden Tiger Moth

Index

About the Author/Illustrator

Todd Telander is a naturalist/illustrator/ artist living in Walla Walla, Washington. He has studied and illustrated wildlife since 1989, while living in California, Colorado, New Mexico, and Washington. He graduated from the University of California at Santa Cruz with degrees in biology, environmental studies, and scientific illustration and has since illustrated numerous books and other publications, including other FalconGuides and FalconGuides' Scats and Tracks series. His wife, Kirsten Telander, is a writer, and he has two sons, Miles and Oliver. His work can be viewed online at toddtelander.com or at telandergallery.com.